Joseph John Gurney

Thoughts on habit and discipline

Joseph John Gurney

Thoughts on habit and discipline

ISBN/EAN: 9783337869243

Printed in Europe, USA, Canada, Australia, Japan

Cover: Foto ©ninafisch / pixelio.de

More available books at **www.hansebooks.com**

THOUGHTS

ON

HABIT AND DISCIPLINE.

BY

JOSEPH JOHN GURNEY.

"Since Custom is the principal magistrate of man's life, let men by all means endeavour to obtain good customs."—*Lord Bacon.*

"The present world is peculiarly fit to be A STATE OF DISCIPLINE, for our improvement in virtue and piety."—*Bishop Butler.*

PHILADELPHIA:
HENRY LONGSTRETH.
No. 1314. CHESTNUT STREET.
1871.

PREFACE.

AMIDST many more serious avocations, the composition of the present work has been the pleasant occupation of occasional leisure hours. Little as it is laboured, and capable as it is of much improvement, I am induced to publish it, in the hope that it may be of *some* use to the lately risen, and now rising generation.

It consists of three divisions. The FIRST contains general remarks on the nature and operation of HABIT and DISCIPLINE; it is the philosophy of the subject, though in a low sense of the term, and in a very familiar guise. The SECOND relates to BAD HABIT—that grand instrument in the hand of Satan, for enslaving, enchaining, and finally destroying mankind: the THIRD, to GOOD HABIT, which is the appointed means, under the natural and moral government of God, and in connexion with a providential scheme of DISCIPLINE, for our improvement in ability, knowledge, wisdom, and virtue.

Good Habit is considered in its application, *first*, to the movements and uses of the body; *secondly*, to art—that useful result of the joint exercise of body and mind; *thirdly*, to intellectual capacities and pursuits; *fourthly*, to morals; and *fifthly*, to religion.

Heartily do I desire that those who are now in the early vigour of their bodily and mental powers, may become subject, in all things, to the salutary power of Good Habit. Under the influence of the Holy Spirit, which can alone change and sanctify the heart of man, they will find in the friendly sway of this " magistrate of man's life' —this genial nurse and mistress of our faculties— a preparation for all that is useful and honourable in time, and for all that is pure and joyous in eternity.

CONTENTS.

CHAPTER I.

ON THE NATURE OF HABIT AND DISCIPLINE.

	PAGE
SECTION I.—On the Capacities of Animals, including Habit	7
SECTION II.—On Habit in Man	37
SECTION III.—On Passive Impressions, and Active Principles	67

CHAPTER II.

ON BAD HABIT.

On Bad Habit	96

CHAPTER III.

ON GOOD HABIT.

SECTION I.—General Principles of Education	127
SECTION II.—On Good Habits of Body	147
SECTION III.—On Good Habits of Art	159
SECTION IV.—On Good Habits of Intellect	171
SECTION V.—On Good Moral Habits	205
SECTION VI.—On Good Religious Habits	262

THOUGHTS

ON

HABIT AND DISCIPLINE.

CHAPTER I.

ON THE NATURE OF HABIT AND DISCIPLINE.

SECTION I.

On the Capacities of Animals, including Habit.

For every living creature—from man down to the lowest reptile—the Creator and Lord of the universe has ordained some particular way of life; and this is determined partly by the capacities of the animal, and partly by the circumstances in which he is placed. The outward appointment and the inward character are "set over" one against the other; and the correspondence between them affords countless proofs both of design and benevolence in the Deity.

The fitness of this lower world to the nature

and needs of the animals which dwell upon it. and especially to those of man, may be traced in a multitude of particulars. The rotation of the earth on its axis, and the consequent alternations of day and night, are just suited to living creatures which require corresponding changes of activity and rest, of waking and sleeping. Our organs of breathing would be of no use had the earth no atmosphere; or had her atmosphere been water instead of air, or air differently composed. Were the air all oxygen, should we not be all on fire? Were it all nitrogen, should we not perish in a moment? Were it incapable of receiving rays of light, what would become of our seeing? Had it no faculty of undulation, where would be our hearing?

It is perfectly conceivable that water, instead of being a flowing liquid, capable of evaporation, might have been stiff like jelly, or aëriform like steam. In either case, where would have been the life of myriads of fishes?—where the fertility of the globe?—where either the meat or the drink of its inhabitants? The surface of the earth might have been all rock, so that no vegetable could grow upon it; or so soft as to be incapable of supporting the foot of man. Who does not perceive that the variety of nature coincides with the *scope* of our animal capacities? If there were no flowers, the powers of smell would yield but little pleasure; and if the flowers produced no honey, the instinct of the bee would be useless. Were nature colourless, where would be the delights of vision? Were she clothed in scarlet instead of green, how soon would our vision be destroyed!* Were the globe, on which we dwell, of a greater bulk than it is at present, so as to exert a stronger attraction towards the moving forms which pervade its surface, all these living creatures would immediately become heavier than they now are. They would walk or run like persons who have lead in their shoes, or who are wearily forcing their way through almost impermeable clay. Were our globe, on the contrary, diminished in bulk, its inhabitants would lose a corresponding proportion of their weight. The stoutest trees would be quickly uprooted, and animals, never made for flight, would be dancing about like feathers in the air. The whole face of nature would become frivolous and unstable. Between the present bulk of the globe, and the actual form and

---

* Many of these particulars, and others of a similar nature, are mentioned in *Dick's Christian Philosopher*, a liltle work well worthy of general attention.

strength of the living creatures upon its surface there is an evidently designed coincidence — a perfect balance — a measured and absolute accordance.

While these, and a thousand other examples, afford a clear evidence, that God has framed this material world with a view to the happiness of its appointed inhabitants, it is not to be forgotten that the world was *first* created, and *afterwards* peopled with living and sentient creatures. It is, therefore, more especially to our present purpose, to consider those inherent capacities by which the various tribes of animals are themselves adapted to their way of life, and to the circumstances with which they are surrounded.

It may not be unprofitable for us to trace some of these capacities in structure—in organic action—in sensation—in instinct, and *in the faculty of habit.*

1. " I will praise thee," said David, " for I am fearfully and wonderfully made: marvellous are thy works, and that my soul knoweth right well: my substance was not hid from thee when I was made in secret, and *curiously wrought* in the lowest parts of the earth..... in thy book all my members were written which in continuance were fashioned, when as yet there was none

of them!"* The inspired writer, though probably but little acquainted with the wonders of anatomy, appears to have been well aware that the mechanism of the human frame affords a direct evidence of the skill of a Creator. But it is not only the delicacy and beauty of the machine—it is the obvious suitability of the whole to the purposes of life, and of its particular parts to their respective functions—it is mechanism with an end in view, and successful in accomplishing that end, which more abundantly proves the wisdom and goodness of our Maker. How curious and scientific is the structure by which the eye is fitted for seeing, the ear for hearing, the lungs for breathing, the stomach for digesting, and the tongue, with all its multitude of muscles and nerves, both for tasting and talking! How admirably is the brain protected by the interwoven bones of the skull, and the vital marrow by the studied machinery of the spine! When we perceive that the ball of the shoulder is tied to the socket in which it moves, by a strong ligament, we cannot for a moment doubt the *final* cause— that the shoulder may not be exposed to dislocation. And who shall say that the procuring cause

---

* Psalm cxxxix. 14—16.

is not equally discoverable? It is the finger of the Most High—it *can be* nothing else.

This subject, however, is most clearly illustrated when we compare the structure of one animal with that of another. To man, who is made for an upright posture, a long neck would be only a source of misery and danger; but quadrupeds, which maintain the horizontal position, and find their food on the ground, require a neck proportioned to the length of their legs—and such a neck is given them. Some idle theorist may imagine that this length of neck, in the horse or the deer, is the effect of protrusion, and was originally produced by the appetency of the creature. But what appetency—what tendency of the head downward—could produce the strong cartilaginous bands, running on either side of the vertebræ, by which, in these and other animals, the neck is strengthened, and enabled to support and lift up the head? Why is this band given to the animals who need it, and withheld from the human species which needs it not?

Every one must perceive that the foot of man and the hoof of the horse are destined for the land; the wings of birds for the air; the fins of fishes for the waters. Why is the fish furnished with a tail, which at once propels him like a paddle, and guides him like a rudder? Because God has determined that he should *move in the waters*. The Creator has also ordained that he should *see in the waters;* and for this purpose the crystalline humour of his eye is created *globular* —a form indispensable to the due concentration of the rays of light in so dense a medium. If we who live in air were furnished with eyes of the same form, the beauties of nature would be lost upon us—our vision would be utterly confused. What can account for the difference, but the design of Omnipotent benevolence?

When Humboldt beheld a magnificent condor, floating through the rarified atmosphere which surrounds the highest tops of the Andes, he could scarcely do otherwise than observe, that the strength and length of its wings corresponded with the size of its body; and he might probably call to mind that such a flight would have been impossible, had not his body, like that of other birds, contained cavities filled with air, and bones remarkable for their *hollowness* as well as strength? This peculiarity in the structure of birds is most clearly indicative of design. So also is their mode of gestation; if this were the same as that of quadrupeds, the flight of the parent bird would be often and long prevented; but the weight of a single light egg offers no impediment to her passage through the air.

It is necessary for the life and comfort of the whale, the seal, and the walrus, that without any effort of their own, and in spite of the weight of their flesh, they should be rendered buoyant in the water. For this purpose they are furnished with a thick stratum, under their skin, of light fat or blubber. Nor is it to be forgotten that the very substance which qualifies these creatures for their own element, affords abundance of oil for the use of man.

The hot and sandy deserts which are the native region of the camel, can have had no tendency to produce those reservoirs at the bottom of his stomach, which he fills with water, and then draws that water, when he pleases, for the quenching of his thirst. Yet were it not for that provision, he would often be a martyr to the climate to which he belongs; and would moreover become comparatively useless to mankind.

What can be more especially adapted to the need of the fish, than the air-bladder within him, which helps to support him in the water, and which he has the power of contracting when he wishes to sink, and of dilating when it is his will to rise? Can the element in which he lives have any tendency to form this curious organ, or must we trace its existence to the hand of the Creator? The waters might flow through the interstices of a fowl's foot forever, and never produce the web which at once connects and separates her toes, and enables her to swim with ease and dexterity. Paley justly remarks that the web-foot, the long and flexible neck, the spoon-bill, the downy breast, and the grass-digesting stomach of the swan, who floats on the surface of the pool, and feeds on the weeds which grow at its bottom, are all made in relation one to another, and in their union, precisely supply the needs of the animal.

The bills and beaks of the various species of birds are exactly adapted to their respective methods of obtaining food; but in these long and often crooked projections, teeth would be at once useless and inconvenient. Now carnivorous birds have no need of any contrivance for grinding their food; for they tear the flesh with their beaks, and digest it without difficulty. But how stands the case with birds which feed on grain, such as the common fowl, the turkey, or the pigeon? Their gastric juice refuses to act on the hard unbroken corn—their food must therefore be ground. And how is the object effected?

Not by teeth, which would only spoil their bills, but by the gizzard—a powerful muscle, furnished with rough folds which rub against each other, and reduce the grain to small particles, as mechanically as the stones of a mill.*

The eyes of various species of fly are so fixed in one position, that these insects have no power to turn the pupil towards an object. The inconvenience which might have arisen from this peculiar structure is prevented by a most elaborate mechanism; for the organ is composed of a vast multitude of minute lenses, through which the animal is enabled to perceive objects in every direction. The number of these lenses in the eye of a dragon-fly, has been found to be 12,000, and in that of a butterfly, 17,000.†

The whole race of Hemipterous insects abstract the juices of plants or animals by " means of a hollow grooved beak, often jointed, and containing three bristle-formed lancets." These lancets, "at the same time that they pierce the food, apply to each other so accurately as to form one air-tight tube, through which the little animals suck up their repast; thus forming a pump, which, more

---

* See *Paley's Natural Theology*, p. 287.

† *Id.*, p. 280. *Kirby and Spence, Introduction to Entomology*, vol. iii. p. 495.

effective than ours, digs the well from which it draws the fluid."*

The examples which have now been cited, and a multitude of others which might easily be collected, afford abundant proofs that the capacity of animals in point of *structure*, is fitted with great exactness to their appointed way of life; and that as the various kinds of living creatures differ one from another in circumstance, so, and so *precisely*, they differ in organization. Equally evident is it that these peculiarities of structure could never have arisen from any tendency or appetency in the animals themselves, and can be reasonably ascribed only to the wisdom and skill of an omnipotent Creator.

2. From structure, the inquirer into nature naturally proceeds to involuntary mechanical motion, and organic action. The exquisite machinery of the bodies of animals would be of no use for the purposes of life, did not their hearts perpetually beat, their blood perpetually circulate, and their lungs perpetually breathe. What would preserve us from death and putrefaction, were there not an unceasing action maintained by our stomach, our biliary ducts, our

---

* *Kirby and Spence, Introduction to Entomology,* vol. i. p. 398.

lacteals, our absorbents, and our nerves? And what could preserve these motions and actions from irregularity and disorder, did they depend on our own capricious will and care? Better things, surely, are provided for the creatures of his hand, by that gracious Being who, in the first place, forms their material frame; in the second place, sets their vital organs in motion; and lastly, maintains the *continual working* of the machine, until the moment arrives when, by his own resistless decrees, they die and return to the dust.

Here it may be well to remark, in passing, that those principles of creative wisdom to which we have hitherto adverted, are displayed (though under a different modification) in the vegetable as well as in the animal kingdom. There is a certain degree of analogy between the structure of animals and that of plants, and both these systems of organized matter display the hand of matchless art, the mind of unrivalled science. There is moreover a comparative anatomy to be remarked in vegetables as well as animals; the peculiar structure of each species being obviously adapted to its appointed way of life; and to the external circumstances in which it is placed. Again, in the germination, growth, blossoming and fructification of vegetables; in the functions of their pores, in the motion of their sap, in their method of drinking up water, and of breathing in and exhaling air — we cannot fail to perceive a resemblance to organic action in animals. Both these branches of the divine economy show forth the ever-present hand of Him who produces and reproduces—who manages and maintains in order—the whole machinery of living things.

3. Ascending one step higher in the scale of that economy, we come to the point which mainly distinguishes the animal from the vegetable kingdom — i. e. *sensation*. The capacity of sensation may be defined as the internal power, by which living creatures perceive the impressions of external things. The appointed instruments through which they receive these impressions, are certain parts of that mechanical structure to which we have already alluded; first, the brain and nervous system; and secondly, the external organs of sense. These things are in a wonderful manner set over against each other. Notwithstanding all the perfection of their structure, blind would be the eye, deaf the ear, tasteless the tongue, and senseless the skin, were not animals furnished with a brain for a sensorium, and with nerves for feelers; and utterly useless

would be the *whole* of this machinery, were there not under it all, the mysterious principle of sensitive existence, hidden from the scrutiny either of the eye or of the understanding, and to be regarded only as the immediate gift of God.

Now, while the inward power of sensation, considered as one of the ordinances of the Almighty, is a subject worthy of deep contemplation, it is no less interesting to reflect on the five distinct channels through which this single faculty is brought into action — the touch, the taste, the smell, the sight, and the hearing. How definite is each of these senses in its own nature and character; and if denied by Providence, how impossible to be acquired, or even conceived! Yet how exactly are they severally fitted to the way of life ordained for the conscious inhabitants of the planet on which we dwell!

It is a delightful evidence of the *benevolence* of our Creator, that all our organs of sense are so framed as to be productive of pleasure. Not one bone, or muscle, or nerve, indeed, has ever been discovered, in any kind of animal, of which the natural tendency is the infliction of pain on its possessor—all are made to produce pleasurable sensations. True, indeed, it is that each of our five senses may be grievously offended; that the organs of animal bodies are capable of derangement and disease; and that the destruction of one living creature by another, is one of the laws through which an inscrutable Providence maintains the order of nature. But while, in the sufferings which are thus occasioned, we may perhaps trace one mark of a fallen and degenerate world, it is nevertheless obvious, even here, that the happiness of conscious living creatures is the *object* of the divine economy: pleasure is the rule, and pain only the exception.

The law of mutual destruction, in the lower animal creation, is, indeed, the law of life. Were that law reversed, and were these sentient creatures left to the slow operation of disease and decay, the sufferings of those animals which now exist would be vastly aggravated; pestilence would spread on every side, and the pleasure of existence itself would soon be fearfully curtailed. Who can listen to the songster of the grove, or to the lark which carols in high air—who can witness the smooth and easy flight of myriads of birds; the happy gliding rapidity of countless fishes; the dance of millions of insects in the sunbeam,— without confessing that great are the pleasures which their Creator has bestowed upon them—

that the painful but unforeseen stroke which may soon consign them to nonentity, is as a cipher in comparison with the unreckoned sum of their enjoyment?

While the five senses are the common property of the generality of animals, the *proportionate strength* in which they are severally imparted, corresponds with the peculiar need of each particular species. In man, indeed, they all maintain an even standard of excellence; but who cannot trace the marks of adapting wisdom and watchful benevolence, in the protected and limited vision of the mole, in the far-seeing eye of the eagle, in the quick hearing of the hare, and in the vivacious smelling of the hound?

4. The fourth leading feature in the capacities of animals, is one which indicates, with peculiar clearness, the all-pervading mind, the ever-acting hand of Deity. That feature is instinct.

Among the things "little upon the earth," yet "exceeding wise," the writer of Proverbs makes mention of the *ant* and the *spider;** and the discoveries of modern naturalists fully confirm this character. Most of the various species of ants are celebrated for their skill in building

---

* Prov. xxx. 24—28.

subterraneous cities; and nothing can exceed the industry and watchfulness, with which they carry on their masonry, and tend the young of their queen. " Every evening, an hour before sun-set they regularly remove the whole brood, together with the eggs and pupæ, to cells situated in the lower part of the nest, where they will be safe from the cold; and in the morning, they as constantly remove them again toward the surface of the nest."* In a well-stocked nest, or *city*, the brood will amount to about 8,000 in number, and the whole of this multitude is fed by the working ants several times in the day, with a viscid fluid which they inject into their mouths individually.† It is a curious circumstance that ants possess the power of mutual communication, so as to be able to give notice to each other of the approach of some hostile tribe, and of issuing their commands to the servants of the colony. The *noiseless touch* appears with them to serve the purpose of man's vociferous tongue.

The white ants of tropical climates (insects of about a quarter of an inch in length) erect domes of prodigious strength and thickness and several feet high. These domes are furnished with

---

* *Kirby and Spence*, vol. i. p. 367. † *Id.* p. 368.

vaults, passages, and cells, suited for the stowage of the young, and for a variety of other purposes. Were we to erect houses of the same proportionate height in relation to the length of our bodies, they would be fifteen times as high as the monument in London!*

The thread of a spider, although little more than just perceptible to the human eye, is spun with astonishing skill, and is, in fact, a cable, composed of four thousand cords.† Supported by this wondrous manufacture, the spider requires no wings, and can attach herself, without difficulty, to the "palaces of kings." And what can be more curiously artificial than the nets which these animals hang up in convenient places in order to catch their prey—sometimes formed in meshes, and sometimes composed geometrically of diverging radii, filled up with a beautiful series of concentric circles?‡

But the wisdom of the ant and the spider is not their own. Each practises her art by a kind of inspiration, without the least knowledge of its rules; and while their energy is excited by appetite, or even prompted by intention, they can be regarded only as the blind executors of their

---

* See *Library of Entertaining Knowledge*, "Insect Architecture," p. 287. † *Kirby and Spence*, vol. i. 107. ‡ *Id.* p. 410.

Creator's will. Not indeed that we are to consider them as mere machines set to work, and kept in motion, by an immediate impulse of divine power, but rather as gifted with certain capacities which adapt them to the circumstances in which God has placed them, and which they are enabled to exercise *spontaneously*. Both the propensity and the power are bestowed on the animal, and form part of its constitution; but the art or science displayed in their methods of carrying their purposes into effect, is not their own. It belongs *only* to God.

Instinct is a faculty incapable of being improved by education. It operates without the force of example, without the instruction of parents, without the formation of habit.

From generation to generation, from age to age, without teaching, and without alteration, either for the better or the worse, the various tribes of animals pursue their respective functions, and exercise the arts of which God has made them capable. The human infant, like the young of lower animals, seeks the breast of its mother, and forms its lips for suction. The silk-worm, to all appearance one of the meanest of grubs, constructs its warm cocoon, and spins its thousand feet of thread, with a delicacy and ingenuity which man cannot rival. The migratory birds behave as if they were weather-wise, and skilled in nautical science; they have something within them, which teaches them when to leave one part of the world, and how to find their way to another. A young pair of linnets or thrushes, let loose from a cage in which they have been confined from their birth, will build their nests in the same situations, with the same materials, and with the same skill and symmetry, as their forefathers did before them. The domestic hen, a dull bird in other respects, would appear to be well acquainted with the theory of heat; for she turns her eggs with the greatest accuracy, so that every part of them may partake of the genial warmth of her body.

Birds which feed on snails or shell-fish, will lift them to a considerable height in the air, and then let them fall on stony places that the shells may be broken, and their prey laid open.

One kind of bee displays the art of a carpenter, a second, that of a mason, a third, that of an upholsterer. The beavers, who set us an example of peaceable social life, are skilful sawyers, builders, and engineers. By gradual and united efforts, they often fell a tree of large dimensions, and always in such a manner that it falls in the right direction. The vast dams which by this and other means they raise across rivers, and which secure for them a pool to dwell in, are formed on the most scientific principles, and are furnished with sloping holes, (contracted or enlarged as occasion requires,) which carry off the surplus water. Their houses are built with admirable firmness against the banks of the river, and are plastered with the greatest neatness; they are provided with doors of entrance or egress towards both land and water, with stories and chambers suited to a family, and with carpets of leaves and branches.*

In order, however, to form a just notion of the operation of instinct, nothing can be more to our purpose, than to reflect for a few moments on the wonders of the honey-comb. Were we to inquire of the geometer, into what *equal* and *similar* figures a plane can be divided, so that all insterstices should be avoided, he would presently tell us that there exist only three such figures —the equilateral triangle, the square, and the regular hexagon; and were we further to ask him, which of these figures would afford the greatest strength, and the most ample room for stowage,

---

* See *Rees' Cyclop.* art. "Castor."

he would reply—" the last of the three." Now this is precisely the figure which the common hive-bee has adopted for her cell. The plane presented to the eye by the section of a honey-comb, is divided, with the utmost exactness, into regular hexagons; and these are so arranged with respect to each other, as to insure the greatest possible degree of stability. The angular bottom of each cell rests on the partition between two other cells, and thus is furnished with a firm buttress on either side.

Our next question must be addressed not to the mere disciple of Euclid, but to the profound mathematician. Supposing a space of solid measurement to be composed of hexagon cells, at what precise angle ought the three planes which compose the bottom of a cell to meet, so as to effect the greatest possible saving of labour and material? The celebrated Maclaurin has determined this question by a fluxionary calculation; and has proved that the angle required is precisely that in which the three planes at the bottom of a cell, in the honey-comb, do actually meet.*

From these facts it seems impossible to avoid deducing one of two inferences; either that the

---

* See *Dr. Hancock on Instinct*, p. 19.

bee is a proficient in superficial and solid geometry, and even in high mathematics, or that she is guided in her work and qualified for its instinctive performance, by the Father and Fountain of science. But the art displayed in the honey-comb is no less admirable than the science. What means the architectural perfection of this insect-edifice? What the even and unfailing measurement of all its parts? It seems impossible to account for these effects, either by the structure of a bee's body, or by the powers of its mind. If so, we must ascribe them immediately to the wisdom and power of him by whom the bee is created.

"Profound geometer, who taught the bee
To mimic science, and to rival thee,
With even hexagons to fill the plane—
Thus ample room with utmost strength to gain;
Nor fill the plane alone; through all the mass
No waste of substance, and no loss of space;
Each cell descending in the angle true,
That great Maclaurin by his fluxions knew?
. . . . . The appointed customs of each busy kind,
Display the working of thy master-mind;
Fountain of science, spring of all that's wise,
Thy moving power their energy supplies . . . . .
Wisdom of God, high partner of his throne.
The Father's pleasure—with the Father one,
From thee of beauty flow the varied streams,
With marks of thee exuberant nature teems.
Thy influence spreads above, around, below—
The best philosophy is THEE to know."

Before we leave this branch of our subject, there is one additional point which requires to be noticed—a point which obviously confirms the view now taken. To a certain extent, instinct is capable of accommodation, and changes with the circumstances of the animal. For example, if the young of birds be exposed in a cage, beyond the time when, according to the usual course of nature, they cease to be the objects of parental care, the mother bird will continue to attend to them —will still display her affection by supplying them with provision. Not long since, a turkey-cock, in the neighbourhood of London, hatched the eggs of its dead hen, and afterwards performed the whole maternal office of nursing and protecting the young brood. Again, in countries infested with monkeys, birds which, in other regions, build in bushes or clefts of trees, suspend their nests upon slender twigs, and by this device elude the rapacity of their enemies—a practice adopted by the youngest pairs, as well as by the more experienced. Thus, also, spiders are observed to change their method of attack and capture, so as to suit the size and character of the different insects on which they feed. These curious variations display, in a remarkable manner, the *pliant* hand of an ever-watchful Providence.

5. The accommodation of instinct, however, although perceptible in a variety of examples, does not appear to be the means most generally employed by the Author of nature for adapting his animal creation to *change of condition and circumstance.* For this purpose, he has implanted in living creatures the faculty of *habit,* through which they obtain an increased facility in performing particular actions, by means of frequently repeating them.

This faculty, which is no less indicative of the wisdom of the Creator, no less inexplicable on the principles of the atheist, than instinct itself, is by no means easy to be traced in the smaller and more inconspicuous tribes—insects, for example. But in creatures of a larger size, whose actions are more easily noticed, it becomes sufficiently apparent, especially in connection with the change which every animal must undergo from youth to maturity. The half-fledged bird is in some measure under the instruction, as well as the care of its parent; and it is by repeated attempts— its wings and feathers growing the while—that it forms the habit of flying. While a prisoner in the nest, it wholly depends on the parent for sustenance; but as its range of liberty and power increases, it becomes habituated to procure food for itself. Birds which sing learn their art by degrees, and are often known to practise it under parental tuition. The powers of motion in young quadrupeds, and their ability to seek and eat the food of the grown-up animal, appear to be formed in like manner, not merely by the growth of their members, but chiefly by that repeated exercise of them, which renders the action easy, and by degrees fixes the custom.

Nor can we confine the influence of habit in dumb animals, to the period of their growth. With beasts as well as man, sagacity and prudence are often the results of continued *experience*. A horse, accustomed to the field, is well acquainted with the extent of his own powers, and will cautiously avoid a leap which is above his force and ability. An old greyhound will trust the more arduous part of the chase to her younger companions, and while she avoids fatigue, will gain her object by meeting the hare in her doubles.

It is a curious fact, that just in proportion as the lower animals are brought under the care of their lordly superior, *man*, they lose the faculty of instinct, and gain that of habit; and although it may not always be easy to trace the influence of habit, in the natural actions of animals, it becomes abundantly evident in the process of domestic training. This remark, however, is intended to apply rather to those animals which are the servants of man, for continued use or amusement, than to those which he keeps and nurtures, only for his table; for the latter, while their powers of instinct decay, generally appear to gain nothing in return, but an increase of flesh. But to watch the mental operations, simple and limited as they are, of the horse, the dog, or the elephant; to mark the effect produced on these animals by a kind and persevering discipline; to observe the docility with which they learn to renounce their natural propensities, and to adopt a course of actions useful to man; to trace the change from difficulty to ease, and from pain to apparent pleasure, in the performance of these actions—is one of the most delightful studies of the naturalist and the metaphysician.

There can be no doubt that the natural tendency of the pointer or setter is to pursue his game without interruption, and it may probably suit him at times to crouch on the ground, in concealment, that he may spring upon it the more surely. But his systematic use of this method, and his steady continuance in a position of restraint until his master overtakes him, and destroys the prey in his stead, is plainly an affair of education and habit. The elephant is not only subjected to military discipline, but is trained without difficulty to the arts of peace. " He lades a boat in a river with surprising dexterity, carefully keeping all the articles dry, and disposing them so judiciously, that their arrangement seldom needs to be changed. In raising wheeled carriages, heavily laden, up an acclivity, he pushes the carriage forward with his front, advances, supports it with his knee, and renews the effort. When dragging a beam of wood along the ground, he removes obstacles to make it run smoothly and easily."*

A friend of mine was in possession of a tortoise which, although accustomed, during the summer, to live abroad in his fields, was sure to seek an asylum, as winter approached, by his master's fireside. Every day, however, at a certain time, he sallied forth in search of food and exercise; and after ranging for two or three hours, returned with the greatest regularity, to his place of warmth and safety. " A few years ago, there was shown at Exeter Change, London, an old monkey, who, having lost his teeth, used, when nuts were presented to him, to take a stone in his hand,

* Dr. Hancock on Instinct, p. 94.

and crack them one by one; thus using means to accomplish his purpose as well as we do."*

These examples, and many others of a similar character, are sufficient to prove that the habits formed by domesticated animals are not purely physical. They are obviously connected with the association of ideas, and involve memory, and possibly some limited degree of the power of reasoning. Their tempers and dispositions also are subject to the influence of custom, and are capable of training and improvement. How often do they form habits of affection, gratitude, and faithfulness, towards those who have the care of them! It would be difficult to find, even in our own species, more affecting examples of attachment and fidelity, than in the elephant, who died of grief, after he had accidentally killed his keeper, and in the dog who watched for three months, over the remains of his master, among the rocks of Helvellyn.

As a general rule, it is evident that where instinct is the main characteristic of an animal, and is left to exert its native sway, there habit has only a very partial influence; and that on the contrary, where instinct gives place to the

---

* Vid. *Rees' Cyclop.* art. "Instinct."

glimmerings of reason, and is weakened by taming and discipline, there habit becomes a ruling and pervading principle. The more intelligent the animal—the greater its power of associating ideas—the less it stands in need of instinct, and the more it becomes capable of forming habits. Above all, in man, in whom reason reigns, there are but small traces of pure instinct, and these belong chiefly to his infancy. But *use*, as I shall soon proceed to show, is his second nature.

On the review of the several points detailed in the present section—of the wondrous exactness with which inanimate nature is suited to the needs of living creatures—of the fitness of their respective capacities to the way of life appointed for each of them; in structure, in organic action, in sense, and in instinct—and lastly, of the method in which, through the faculty of habit, they are adapted to every successive change in their condition—we may well feel constrained to join with the Psalmist in his words of wonder and praise; "O Lord, how manifold are thy works; in wisdom hast thou made them all..... The glory of the Lord shall endure forever; the Lord shall rejoice in his works!"*

---

* Ps. civ. 24—31.

SECTION II.

On Habit in Man.

WHILE we are led by a variety of facts, familiar to the most cursory observer, to ascribe to many of the lower animals such a glimmering of reason as leads them to adopt means in order to accomplish *ends*, we must not forget that the line which separates them from the human species is broad and impassable. Although, in the first place, individuals among them, under the fostering care of man, form many useful habits, and experience some enlargement of faculty, they have no means of transmitting these advantages to their posterity; they are capable of no generic improvement. The race of elephants, of dogs, or of horses, in point of knowledge and endowment, is precisely the same now as it was a thousand years ago — a fact, which, although closely connected with their want of language, can by no means be ascribed to it. This want must rather be regarded as a *second* mark of the narrow limits within which the Creator has circumscribed their mental faculties; for we know that some animals possess organs which enable them to pronounce articulate sounds.

Of the higher exercises of mind, such as reflection, abstraction, and generalization, and of any but the shortest processes of reasoning, they are, in all probability, wholly incapable; and this conclusion obviously agrees with their habits of life. For their bodies they demand no clothing, and for their food no cooking; the erect posture, so suitable to rational beings, is for the most part strange to them. Expressive as their looks and sounds sometimes are, they are capable only of a very low degree of social communion. Above all, while they are under the natural government of God, and blindly obey its laws, they are incapable of knowing, and therefore of worshipping, their Creator. They have no lot or part in his moral government. They have no law of righteousness written on their hearts, and therefore no responsibility. They are subject to no bar of inquiry— to no tribunal of divine justice.

Satisfactorily to account for their consciousness, and for their measure of mental power, on the principles of mere materialism, does indeed appear to be impossible. But we have no reason to believe that their minds are formed for immortality, and the holy Scriptures, by giving no countenance whatsoever to such a notion, may at least be said to *indicate* the contrary. They do, indeed, go further; they contrast "the spirit of the beast that goeth downward to the earth," with "the spirit of man that goeth upward;"* they speak with peculiar emphasis of the "beasts that *perish*;"† and the divine grant which they record, of animals to man, *for his food,* in itself affords a strong presumptive evidence that these living creatures are no heirs of eternity.‡

But man was "created in the image" and "after the likeness" of God§—a declaration which involves the doctrine, elsewhere unfolded in Scripture, that an immortal spirit is his portion. He is appointed to rule over the lower animals. His soul is so enlightened by reason, that he can be taught to exercise all its purer and loftier powers. He is capable of an indefinite degree of mental cultivation, and can transmit to his descendants all his improvements in manners, all his discoveries in art or science. He can clothe his thoughts in language; and his speech is

---

* Eccl. iii. 21. † Psalm xlix. 12.
‡ Gen. ix. 3.   § Gen. i. 26.

capable of an almost infinite variety. This pliant system of audible and legible signs, not only affords him an endless scope in the acquirement of knowledge, but supplies a machinery for thought and reflection, as useful for these purposes, as arithmetical figures, algebraic signs, and logarithms, are in mathematics. Above all, he is capable of fearing, loving, and worshipping his Creator, and of receiving the illumination of God's Holy Spirit. He is furnished with a moral faculty; he is called to virtue and to glory; and in a future and eternal world, he must render to the Judge of all flesh the account of his stewardship.

There is one feature, however, in the constitution and circumstances of mankind, which on the present occasion demands a particular notice. Of all the creatures of God, with which we are acquainted, he is the most exposed to change of condition, and the most capable of corresponding alterations in character and practice.* Just in proportion to the scope of his rational and moral

---

* Some of the insect tribes may perhaps be considered as affording an exception to this remark; but the caterpillar, the grub, and the butterfly, can scarcely be regarded as one and the same creature. We describe them by different names, and may fairly regard them as different creatures, springing one from the other.

faculties, are the versatility of his constitution and the variations in his way of life. And in a preeminent degree it is the law of his nature, that one stage of his being should serve as a preparation for another. On a protected and regulated infancy, depends a healthy and happy boyhood; on a boyhood well governed and instructed, the vigour and virtue of early maturity; on that vigour and virtue, the usefulness and stability of middle life; and on these, again, the comfort and tranquillity of age. Above all, under the mercy and grace of God, the present life, rightly spent, is a path-way to the "holiest place of all"—a preparation for the glory and bliss of heaven.

Of what incalculable importance, then, to such a creature as man, is the law of habit—the law ordained by the Author of our nature, that *every exertion, either of body or mind, should become easier by repetition;* that, in other words, *an aptitude and disposition for any action, whether bodily or mental, should be formed in us, by the frequent performance of the action itself.* This is the law by which we are enabled to fall in, by degrees, with every change in our condition; to qualify ourselves for the general purposes of life, and for the peculiar functions of our calling; to store our minds with knowledge; to form our manners, and, with divine aid, to improve and regulate our tempers and dispositions. Finally, this law, under the influence of the Holy Spirit, is applied to its highest purpose, in that process of sanctification, by which the believing and obedient soul is gradually purified from sin, and prepared for the element of a holier world.

Again, how awful is the consideration, that the faculty of habit is capable of being completely misapplied, and of working with undiminished vigour, in an opposite direction!

Why actions become easier in consequence of being repeated, is a question which scarcely belongs to fair metaphysical science. It is, as I have stated above, an ordinance of the Deity, and is no more capable of being explained, except by a direct reference to his will, than the law of gravitation. Our proper business is to attend to facts—to examine the practical effects of this law, and the manner in which it operates—to detect the dangers which attend its perversion—and to point out how it may be best applied to our substantial welfare, in relation both to the present life, and to an eternal future.

1. The subject may, in the first place, be illustrated by a reference to habits simply bodily; for the organs of the body are as much the

subjects of this pervading law, as the capacities of the mind. Some habits of this description are formed at so early a stage of infancy, and become so purely mechanical and involuntary, that they can scarcely be distinguished from original organic actions. The closing of the eyelids, for example, is a habit gradually formed in the infant, by the impulse of light upon the organs of vision; and so perfect does this habit become, that we close our eyelids thousands of times every day, without being aware of the action.

What a lesson may we learn from this single circumstance, respecting the tendency of that mysterious law, which is still the same *in its nature*, whether it be applied to the body or to the mind — to things physical, intellectual, or *moral!*

Just in the same manner in which we become accustomed to perform the useful office of closing our eyelids, and afterwards perform the action without perceiving it, do we sometimes contract a variety of personal habits, which are quite useless, and perhaps deforming. These often arise, in the first instance, from accidental causes, and afterwards, from frequent repetition, become involuntary and mechanical. How often do we perceive in grown up persons some peculiar gait or gesture—some motion of the eye, the mouth, or the hand—which they have learned in boyhood, practise without knowing it, and carry about with them to their dying day!

Other corporeal habits, although familiar in the greatest degree, continue nevertheless to be under the guidance of the will. For example, the use of the teeth in eating, and of the legs in walking. Neither of these practices is original: they are both learned in early life, and are not to be mistaken for mere instincts. What beautiful examples of the effect of habit on the functions of the body—of its power to render difficult exertions easy, and awkward motions graceful, and to convert even pain into pleasure—are afforded us by the experienced swimmer or skaiter?

2. Many of the habits which men are accustomed to form, operate at once on the body and the mind. A curious example of this nature is to be observed in the *art of seeing*—an example which affords a proof that mental as well as bodily functions may, from long custom, be exercised imperceptibly to ourselves. We, of course, ascribe the effect called seeing, to the internal power of vision, in connexion with the outward organ. But to see things as they really are—that is, to

perceive by the sight their true size, their relative positions, and their comparative distances—is a matter of habit, in which (though we are not aware of it) the *mind and the judgment* are full as much concerned as the eye. It is the result of perpetual repetition, and of long experience.

What a countless number of objects, of various sizes and descriptions, does the eye embrace, in what we are accustomed to deem a single act of vision! Yet metaphysicians tell us that all these objects are perceived in succession, and that the sight of each of them, and of every perceptible part of each of them, is preceded by a distinct though unknown exertion of the mind, and of the *will.** This notion, which some persons may regard as purely hypothetical, derives considerable support from the analogy of other human actions, in which the faculties of the mind, and the organs of the body—both under the influence of habit—are known to move on together with astonishing rapidity.

A merchant's clerk, accustomed to add up long lines of figures, employs his eye, his hand, and his mind, in the operation. These keep even pace with each other, as he goes on from figure to

---

* See *Dugald Stewart on the Human Mind*, vol. i. p. 130.

figure, and the rapidity with which they move soon renders him unconscious of that distinct act of his will, by which every step in the calculation is unquestionably preceded.

How rapidly will the ready writer fill the sheet which he is about to transmit to a brother or a friend! What a multitude of muscles, tendons, and nerves, he presses into the service! How almost incalculable the number of distinct motions of the hand, whereby he forms all the characters of which his letter is composed, and with what incredible versatility do his mind and will accompany him in every step of the process! Now every one knows that all these wonders—and wonders they truly may be called—are the simple effect of habit.

In reading aloud, in conversation, in exhortation, in debate, how volubly do we pour forth words! And how little do we dream of the multitudinous fibres in the tongue, which we are keeping in constant motion; or of the voluntary effort of the mind, which precedes every turn and modulation of the sound! Again—nothing can be more curious than the manner in which, under the influence of habit, our thoughts and our words become married to each other, and flow on together in perfect unison.

A due consideration of the habits of art, which for the most part require the joint action of our bodily and mental powers, is indeed of great importance to our present subject. Some of them, such as reading and writing, are adapted to the general use of men; but for the most part they are the means of qualifying us for some peculiar station or service in life. Certain it is that no art can be rightly applied without a practical knowledge of its rules; nor can we forget the advantage to the artificer himself, of a scientific acquaintance with its principles; but it is the influence of habit—it is the sure though gradual effect of repeated trial—which surmounts the difficulties of the work, renders it plain and familiar, and crowns the efforts of the workman with uniform success. Were it not for this pervading law of nature and Providence, the various wants of civilized society could never be supplied. The world would be deprived of the experienced husbandman, the skilful mechanic, the expert mariner, and the dexterous surgeon. We should have no ceiled houses to dwell in, no glass for our windows, no ships for the commerce of nations, no manufactured stuffs, no artificial clothing. By a rapid and untimely change we should presently fall back into the condition of the lowest tribes of savages.

The beneficial effect of custom in works of art, is very conspicuous in the *division of labour*. By this system the faculty which each individual possesses of forming a habit of art, instead of being weakened by distraction, is made to bear, with undivided force, on a particular object. The cutting, the pointing, the silvering, and the heading, of a pin, are severally the single object of a workman's attention. Each person establishes his own habit, and by the combined efforts of all, the article is produced in its perfection.

It has often been remarked that the frequent repetition of an action, not only renders it easy, but engenders in the mind a proneness to perform it. To this feature in the general law of custom, habits of art are considered, by some writers, to offer an exception; but although many of the arts of life are laborious to the performer, and from peculiar causes may sometimes become distasteful, I cannot allow the exception to be valid. It is unquestionably the effect of custom to render exertions of mind or body, which are in the first instance painful as well as difficult, not only easy but pleasant; and no sooner is this pleasure felt, than an inclination is produced in the mind to obtain it—we become more and more attracted to the pursuit. That this is true, as it regards the *fine arts,* every one knows; and with respect to those of a rougher and more toilsome nature, they who willingly submit to that divine decree which demands the sweat of man's brow for the earning of his bread, will find it alleviated by an attendant provision of mercy. Their work will be rendered agreeable, just in proportion as it becomes habitual.

3. The exertion of any one of our intellectual faculties is as much an action of the man, as the motion of our teeth in eating, or of our legs in walking; and such exertion is perpetually taking place in us without any corresponding movement of our outward frame. Hence it follows, according to the general principles of the law of habit, that we are capable of forming many habits of a nature purely intellectual, and these may either afford us important advantages, or involve us in grievous loss and inconvenience. Were mankind more generally sensible of this truth, they would exercise a greater watch over their mental processes, and over the multitude of the thoughts within them!

A few examples of intellectual habits will be sufficient to illustrate the subject.

The power by which the mind *perceives* and *observes* an object which is present to the external organs of sense, and the power by which it afterwards *conceives* the same object, when those organs can no longer reach it, are faculties which grow weaker by neglect, and stronger by cultivation. The habits of accurate perception and observation, and of vivid conception, are all of them of great importance to the purposes of life; and the two former are essential to the last. The more diligent and exact the use which we make of our senses, the stronger and more faithful will be our mental imitations of that which we have already perceived.

The faculty of *attention*, whereby the mind directs itself to any idea which may be presented to it, detains that idea in its passage, examines it carefully, and records it on the tablets of memory, is one which, although a part of our nature, is peculiarly liable to weakness and decay. It may indeed be said, more or less, to lie waste, from neglect, in the mind of almost every man. Nevertheless the habit of attention is capable of being formed and nurtured; and when the faculty of thus applying the mind to its object is strengthened by a daily diligence, the practice of it — fraught with usefulness — becomes comparatively easy. To change the objects of our attention, and to give the whole mind to each object in succession, is another attainment of great use in life, and mainly depends on custom. The ease with which many minds turn from one occupation to another, or in one word, *versatility*, is the result partly perhaps of genius, but chiefly of long engagement in the rapid affairs of life. It is as much the effect of habit, as the ever varying adjustments of a balancer, or the legerdemain of a conjuror.

When we have once received any particular ideas into the mind, we form an acquaintance with them, and on our meeting with them again, we recognize them. When moreover we have met with them repeatedly, and thought of them frequently, our knowledge of them becomes so familiar, that they are often recalled to the mind at a moment's notice. Such is the operation of *memory*, which must therefore be regarded as analogous in its very nature, to the faculty of habit. Certain it is, however, that our power of retaining and recalling ideas is peculiarly subject to the sway of custom; it is soon weakened by disuse, and as readily strengthened by practice. A susceptible, retentive, and ready memory, must indeed be considered as in part depending on physical causes; but to a great extent it is the result, first, of close attention, and secondly, of diligent exercise and frequent recollection.

To ascend from individual objects to abstract ideas, and from particular facts to general truths, is the province and pleasure of the philosopher. These are the means by which he is enabled to arrange and classify nature, and to discover the laws by which she is governed. On the other hand, the man who is engaged in the active business of life, is incessantly occupied with details. He is constantly dealing with individual things, persons, and facts, and can spare but a small portion either of time or thought, for abstracting and generalizing.

The undeviating effect of each of these pursuits — philosophy or business — is to form its corresponding *habit* of mind; and in both cases, the habit requires to be checked by a wholesome counteraction. The philosopher who is not *conversant* with particular facts, and accurate in examining them, will soon fall into false conclusions; and the man of business who forms no general conclusions, will as speedily involve himself in practical mischief.

Reasoning and imagination will supply us with additional examples. The faculty by which we compare our ideas, deduce one proposition from another, and thus make progress in the discovery of truth; and that by which we select from the realities around us, the ideas which strike our fancy, and weave them, at our pleasure, into a new creation, have each a wide range in our nature, and exercise a most important influence over our condition and destiny. Both however bow with submission to the sceptre of habit. Who has not observed the difference between the man in whom the reasoning faculty has long been lulled to sleep, and his neighbour, who delights to employ himself in the weighing of evidence, and in the investigation of truth? How different, again, is the habitual mental complexion of the judge or of the mathematician, from that of the individual who is constantly engaged in weaving the web of fiction or in stringing the gems of poetry!

When a man, long accustomed to calculation and demonstration, can no longer appreciate moral and probable evidence, or loses his relish for the objects of a refined taste, he affords us a teaching evidence that the exclusive pursuit even of very sober studies may be fraught with loss and danger. Such must have been the case with a celebrated mathematician at Cambridge, who is said to have declared that he took no pleasure whatsoever in *Virgil,* "because he *proved* nothing." On the other hand, how imperceptible in its progress, how fascinating in its operation, how weakening to all our better faculties, is an uncontrolled imagination? To strengthen our reasoning powers, and at the same time to confine them within their true limits; and to subdue the imagination, without destroying its use or marring its beauty, are triumphs over the weakness of our nature, which (under the divine blessing) can be achieved only by habit.

The *judgment* and the *taste* are both capable, through habit, either of perversion or improvement. A man of sanguine temperament, and little disposed to cool reflection, will often become so habituated to imprudent counsels, that the most teaching misfortunes will fail to correct his propensity. "Though thou shouldest bray a fool in a mortar among wheat with a pestle, yet will not his foolishness depart from him." So also the man of low tastes, however severely punished, will usually be found to pursue his customary course of degrading pleasure. On the other hand, both these faculties may be cultivated in a right direction. The *gift* of a sound judgment, as well as of a pure and discriminating taste, may be greatly enlarged by experience, and strengthened by habitual exercise.

One more point, connected with the subject of intellectual habits, demands our especial attention. The thoughts of men follow one another in a train, and every thought suggests its successor to the mind. This suggestion arises out of some relation between the two, such as similarity, contiguity in time or place, contrast, cause, and effect, or circumstances of a purely arbitrary or casual nature, with which any idea may have become connected. Although this curious faculty of *suggestion or association* must be regarded as an original principle of our nature, both the pace and the direction of its movements are extremely dependent on habit. Some persons think, as well as speak, with great rapidity; they are practised in that ready perception of the relation of ideas, which leads to a quick and extensive association, and the current of their thoughts flows like a mountain stream. Through the minds of others, thoughts move along at a slow march, and each takes its time in suggesting its successor. So also the *direction* of the train depends on the pursuits of the thinker. The geologist, the painter, and the political economist, are perhaps fellow-travellers through a foreign country, and as they keep close company, the same objects are presented to the senses of each of them; but the first is always thinking on the soil and the strata, the second on the picturesque beauties of the country, and the third on the condition of the inhabitants. On their return home, their respective journals afford a clear evidence of the influence of habit over their mental associations.

The waking hours of every one are necessarily filled with thought; but to think profitably, and to reflect deeply — to dismiss our useless or dangerous thoughts in an instant, and to detain our useful ones on their passage, to examine them with watchful care, and to dive into their hidden relations — these are mental arts of the highest importance to our welfare, and for which, under Providence, we are indebted to exercise and custom.

While, however, it must be allowed that the faculty which we possess of associating our ideas, like all our other powers, is assisted and directed by custom, it is of particular importance to observe, that the operation of habit essentially depends, in many cases, on our original faculty of association.

In connection with every action which we perform, a variety of ideas are linked together;

when the action is repeated, this association is confirmed; and by frequent repetition, it becomes in the greatest degree familiar. The consequence is, that when any circumstance recalls any one of these ideas to us, all the rest rush into our minds, and by their united force, we are again propelled to the action. It is evident therefore that these faculties of our nature act and re-act; and while habit rules over association, as it does over all our other powers, association may safely be regarded as the strength and main-spring of habit.

4. The preceding remarks respecting our rational faculties, and the habits of which they are capable, are sufficient to show the subtle and powerful nature of the human mind. The more, indeed, we reflect on the philosophy of mind, and examine the extent and variety of our intellectual operations, the clearer will become our conviction that we have within us a living principle, destined to survive the wreck of matter, and to endure for ever.

The main distinction, however, of the human soul—the ground of its responsibility, and therefore the strongest internal evidence of its future life of happiness or misery—is the moral faculty by which we are enabled to perceive and understand the law of our God.

God is a holy Being; he has written the law of righteousness on the heart of man, and we have every reason to believe that this internal revelation is a work of that Holy Spirit who has developed the same law, in all its branches and particulars, through the medium of Scripture. The faculty by which the mind of man perceives this law, and is compelled to confess its rectitude, is called the moral sense. This sense enables us to distinguish between right and wrong, and so to form an estimate, in a moral point of view, of the conduct and character of other men; but when it is applied to the more important act of judging our own intentions and actions, it assumes the name of conscience. Conscience, when truly guided by the Holy Spirit, is the representative of God in our bosoms, and ought to reign supreme over all our actions, bodily and mental.

Now it is a consideration of the highest moment, that the law of habit applies to our moral dispositions and conduct, just as certainly as it does to the common movements of the body, and to the exertions of intellectual power. On them *all* it works in the same mysterious manner, and with an equal and uniform efficacy. It is an awful thought that our responsible and moral nature, like every other part of man, is subject to this mistress of our powers, either for good or evil!

In the first place, the conscience itself is as completely liable to the operation of habit, as any other faculty of our nature. It is kept alive by the continual exertion of its power, and by enforcing its decisions on the practice of the man. The more frequent the victories obtained, through the help of the Holy Spirit, by this inward arbiter of our deeds, over the perverse inclinations of the heart, and the more numerous our acts of obedience to its decrees, the greater will become its susceptibility, the quicker and more enlightened its judgments. On the other hand, if conscience speaks in vain, and fails, even on a single occasion, to arrest the course of sin, it is immediately weakened; and after the frequent repetition of defeat, the power of the judge is lost, and weakness ends in death. Such was the condition of those persons of whom the apostle says, they had " their conscience seared with a hot iron"*—a condition from which, without direct divine interposition, there could be no recovery.

Again, by the force of example, education,

---

* 1 Tim. iv. 2.

and habit, the conscience may be led in a right direction; it may be enlightened and strengthened in its support of virtue; or, on the contrary, it may become so strangely perverted, as to be constantly forming erroneous decisions. Never, indeed, can this faculty be so reversed as to approve of evil because it is evil—to countenance falsehood or malice, for example, for its own sake—for this would amount to the utter destruction of the moral principle. But far too quickly may the conscience be taught upon some false plea, and in conformity to its own natural tendency in the fall, to "call evil good, and good evil;" to "put darkness for light, and light for darkness;" to "put bitter for sweet, and sweet for bitter;"* and thus under the pretence of duty, to "draw iniquity with cords of vanity, and sin as it were with a cart rope!"†

In the second place, particular moral qualifications are formed by habit. Behold the man who abounds in benevolence. The quality may be natural to him; or if it be something more than natural, partaking in the nature of true Christian charity, it must be regarded as the effect of grace. In either case, however, the

---
* Isaiah v. 20. † Isaiah v. 18.

large proportion which it occupies in the mental constitution, is inseparably connected with the oft repeated exertions of the quality itself. Behold the man given to covetousness—his niggardly disposition may perhaps be a native tendency, but that tendency has assumed its full-grown form under the influence of repeated acts of parsimony. In the same manner may habits be formed either of submission to authority, or of self-will and impatience of restraint, of pity or of hard-heartedness, of malice or forbearance, of meekness or forwardness, of humility or self-conceit, of love or hatred. Moral qualities become settled in the character, partly by means of exertions of the mind alone—such as good or evil thought, sinful or virtuous intention, plans of corrupt indulgence on the one hand, or wise and holy resolutions on the other. But chiefly are they established through the repetition of overt actions—i. e. through the *practice*—to which these mental operations naturally lead.

Lastly, it is undeniable that the actual moral conduct of every man is formed through the operation of *habit*. If we give way to that unlawful indulgence of our appetites, which is dictated by our fallen nature, sin steals upon us by insensible degrees; each succeeding evil action strengthens the disorder of our mental constitution, and we become vicious by custom. If, on the contrary, we exercise a just control over our passions—if we allow that grace which alone can sanctify, to lead us onward from one act of self-denial to another—the temptation to evil is weakened by degrees, and we form the *custom* of virtue. The thief, the liar, the drunkard, and the murderer, all attain to their acmé of criminality—the merciful, the beneficent, and the holy, all ascend their scale of virtue—by means of the silent, yet sure and effective, influence of *habit*.

Nor can it be denied that in matters which relate exclusively to religion, the sway of habit is still clearly manifest. The forgetfulness of God, and a listless apathy respecting our future and eternal well-being, are constitutional in fallen man, but they are vastly strengthened by habit. Every action performed without regard to God, and every day spent without a thought of heaven and hell, confirms that frame of ungodliness which precedes and bespeaks its awful result—even the eternal separation of the soul from its Creator. On the other hand, the habitual exercise of holy contemplation, fervent prayer, faith, obedience, &c., is the means by which the Christian grows in grace, and is finally prepared for perfect and endless bliss.

It appears, then, that just in proportion to the elevation of man above the lower animals, in point of rational and mental power, is the superior degree in which he is endowed with the faculty of habit, whereby he may be qualified for those numerous and important changes of condition, which belong to his destiny.

This faculty is to be regarded as an original part of our constitution, for which we can account only by a direct reference to the will of the Creator, but of which we may easily understand the nature, and examine the effects. These have now been traced, under several distinct heads.

First, in actions purely bodily—such as the closing of the eyelids, and other involuntary motions, and in the voluntary ones of the teeth, the limbs, &c., in performing their several functions.

Secondly, in the joint action of body and mind, as in seeing *aright;* in writing, reading, and speaking; in studied elocution, and in the whole catalogue of human arts.

Thirdly, in operations entirely mental—for example, perception, conception, attention, memory, abstraction, reasoning, and imagination, judgment and taste; also in the association of ideas, which is itself essential to the law of habit, yet subject to its influence.

Lastly, in moral and spiritual things—in the use or disuse, improvement or perversion, of conscience; in the dispositions of the heart; in good or evil conduct; in the religious or irreligious life.

Two general observations will now bring this section to a conclusion.

First—" if the force of custom, simple and separate, be great," says Lord Bacon, " the force of custom, copulate and conjoined, and collegiate, is far greater; for there example teacheth, company comforteth, emulation quickeneth, glory raiseth: so as in such places, the force of custom is in its exaltation."* It is indeed an obvious truth, that when men are collected in society, there are many causes which promote the easy formation among them of all kinds of habits. The chief cause, however, is *example*, which exerts an amazing influence on all our habits, bodily, intellectual, and moral. The power of imitation, aided as it is by sympathy, is one of the most influential faculties of our nature, and one to the

---

* *Essays*, No. xxxix.

exercise of which there is a universal proneness in our species. Instances which prove the fact abound on every side of us. Who has not observed that peculiarities of manner, voice, and expression, as well as particular lines of thought and opinion, often pervade a complete family circle? The repeated gape of an individual will sometimes excite the yawns of a whole company; and noises or gestures, indicative of approval or disapproval, will spread, like wild-fire, through a large assembly. The painter, the sculptor, and even the poet, form their styles, more or less, on the pattern of their predecessors, and not an art is practised in civilized society, which does not owe much of its progress to the power of copying. Whatsoever, indeed, may be the nature of our pursuits and engagements, we are prone to mould ourselves on the model of other men. In our sentiments, our tastes, and our moral conduct, as well as in our arts and manners, we are still found to be copyists—imitation and sympathy still display themselves as the handmaids and forerunners of habit!

Our second remark relates to the extremely gradual and subtle manner in which our customs are formed. The gesture of body—the mode of thought—the manner of expression—or the line of conduct, steals upon us with imperceptible steps, and before we know it, we have resigned our freedom; we move along in chains, and are no longer the masters of our own actions. The growth of habit in a man is like that of a plant in his garden—silent and impalpable, yet sure and constant; first the stem, then the blossom, and finally, in its season, an abundant crop of fruit, whether wholesome or poisonous, whether sweet or bitter!

SECTION III.

On passive Impressions and active Principles.

THERE is one feature in the law of habit so important in its operation, and, at the same time, so distinct in its nature, that it appears to demand a separate notice. *Our power of passive sensation is weakened by the repetition of impressions, just as certainly as our active propensities are strengthened by the repetition of actions.*

This principle appears to be of very general application—to the organs of the body, to the powers of the mind, to the dispositions of the heart.

A person afflicted with chronic disease, adopts the use of narcotic medicines; but as the doses are repeated, he soon finds that the effect of each of them diminishes: he is therefore obliged to increase the number or quantity of his draughts, in order to make up for the decay of the *passive impression*. For the very same reasons, the snuff-taker is forced, by the tyranny of habit, to recur to his box with an ever-increasing frequency; and the gin-drinker, under a similar stern compulsion, is sure to multiply and enlarge his potations. In all these cases, there is not only a weakening of the bodily organs, but a decay of the mental sensation. The power of the medicine is less and less felt; the pungency of the powder and the fire of the liquor are less and less enjoyed; but the craving is increased, the vacuum is enlarged, the active propensity is wrought up in the constitution, and the man becomes the slave of his habit.

The mental faculties of perception and attention, are both of them prone to fade under the frequent repetition of the same impression, and nothing will counteract the effect thus produced, but the formation of an active habit. The student is awakened out of his slumbers by the alarum at his bedside, and if he forms the *custom* of early rising, the contrivance is successful. Although, as the mornings follow each other, the sound becomes less and less striking, the increasing energies of his new propensity supply, and more than supply, the deficiency. But let him resist the impression of his alarum for a few mornings, and his slumbers will be no more disturbed; its voice will speak in vain, the ear may receive the sound, but the mind will no longer perceive it.

The road over which a man daily travels from his residence to his place of business, happens to lie through beautiful scenery. At first he is delighted with the prospects; but unless he cultivates the *habit* of examining and admiring them, he will soon pass along, almost without perceiving them. His *mental* eye will close upon their beauty.

All men are struck by novelties, whether they are visible substances, or abstract truths; but as the newness of the object, and the freshness of the idea, are lessened by repetition, they lose their power of exciting our *attention*. In order to attend to them properly, we must form a counteracting habit of mental exertion.

Our emotions of passion and feeling are subject to the same rule. What an ardent glow of love is felt by two brothers or sisters, at the moment of their meeting after a long separation, and how appropriately is it represented by the warm and joyful embrace! Yet, in a very short time, such a token of affection would become untimely. Under the influence of continued intercourse, the passive impression is weakened. The resistless emotion subsides into a quiescent and regular state of feeling.

This hint appears to open our way to a general remark of the highest importance—namely, that our best feelings, our holiest desires, our moral virtues, and even our Christian graces, will all be sure to decay, unless the weakening of the passive impression is counteracted by the strengthening of the active principle. A few examples will render the subject clear and familiar.

The feeling of pity is naturally excited in the mind by the appearance of a fellow-creature in pain or distress. But when a multitude of such objects have been presented to our attention, one after another, the sensation is weakened, the pain which such a sight engenders becomes less poignant, and the pity, even of the merciful, grows comparatively cool. By what means then are we to make up for the deficiency? By acts of beneficence—not merely gifts of money, but exertions of mind and body, for the relief of our afflicted fellow-creatures. If the active principle be thus insured, even the passive feeling of pity will never die; the habit of *attention* to the objects which excite it will be established, and benevolence will imbue our mental constitution. On the other hand, if our feelings of pity do not lead us into action, they will fade away with astonishing quickness, and we shall soon become as insensible as stones to the sufferings of others.

Many persons are prone to substitute for the realities of life, a fictitious picture, drawn either by themselves or others, and are satisfied with indulging their benevolence only in imagination. While they take little or no notice of the cries of the poor, or of the sorrows of the prisoner, they will feast on the excitement of a tragedy, and weep over a novel. But there is no greater delusion than this; for of all cold hearts, the heart of the sentimentalist is often found to be the coldest. " Going over the theory of virtue in one's thoughts," says Bishop Butler, " talking well, and drawing fine pictures of it—this is so far from necessarily or certainly conducing to form a habit of it in him who thus employs himself, that it may harden the mind in a contrary course, and render it gradually more insensible: i. e. form a habit of insensibility to all moral considerations."*

Submission to parental authority is a Christian virtue, too often disregarded, but of high practical

---

* *Analogy*, chap. v.

importance. But except the child be accustomed to *acts* of obedience, the mental impressions which give rise to them will always be growing weaker. After a time, the parental command, so often repeated in vain, will scarcely descend into the ear, and will produce no effect upon the mind; and before manhood arrives, there will be as little of the feeling left of subordination or dependence, as in the young of animals, when nature leads them to forsake their dams, and to provide for themselves.

Scenes of death are frequently passing before us in this world of change. The mourners go about the streets, again and again the grave is opened before us, again and again are we called to weep for the loss of a relative or a friend. Such scenes are calculated to excite an awful sense of the shortness of life, and of the vast importance of preparation for eternity. But except we apply our mental powers to the subject, and make a diligent use of these occasions of serious reflection, such scenes will presently lose their effect upon us, and the more we see of death, the less we shall care for its approach.

The importance of filial reverence towards the Almighty, and the duty of worshipping him with the heart, is on all hands confessed. But woe unto those who neglect the religion of the closet, or of the congregation. The impression produced on them by the often recurring proofs of our heavenly Father's love, will grow weaker and weaker, and will soon be reduced almost to nothing. It is the act of solemn waiting upon God, and of communion with him in prayer and praise, when we make " melody" in our " hearts unto the Lord"—it is the diligent performance of all our religious *duties*—by which, under divine grace, the flame of devotion is kept alive in our bosoms, and the habit of godliness established.

Although, however, the gradual weakening of passive impressions exposes us to some temptations, and requires to be met by an opposite influence, it ought by no means to be regarded as a defect in the constitution of our nature. On the contrary, it is a law peculiarly adapted to our need, and affords a remarkable proof of the wisdom and benevolence of our Creator.

That this is a provision of tender mercy, is well understood by the sick man, who has been long accustomed to be racked with pain, and who finds his sufferings tolerable, as they become habitual. It is understood also, by the child of affliction, whose grief is no sooner familiar, than it begins to wane, and who bears his seventh trouble with a quietness and equanimity to which, during his earliest sorrow, he was comparatively a stranger.

The terrors of the ocean are of perpetual recurrence, and continue from year to year unabated. But how rapidly does the impression of them subside in the mind of the sailor! How quickly he finds the sea his proper element! how calm he becomes, from frequent experiment, in the hour of danger! Were the sympathy which the surgeon feels with his patient, when he first performs an operation, to continue without diminution, it would be almost impossible for him to pursue his calling. A dangerous pity would soon prevent all the usefulness of his knowledge and his skill.

Above all, this principle in our nature, when rightly applied, affords a most important aid to virtue. The decay of the passive impression gives an ever-increasing scope for the play of the active habit by which it is surmounted. Courage and self-possession, for instance, are confirmed by frequent experiment and practice; but who does not perceive that in forming these habits of mind, we are assisted by the gradual diminution of the passive feeling of terror? Patience and resignation are doubtless established in the mind through a series of mental acts of submission and long-suffering; but, under the merciful government of our Creator, they are greatly promoted by the decay of our painful sensations.

Afflictions operating on our unsubdued hearts, have a natural tendency to excite a murmuring spirit; but as the mind is steadily turned in submission towards its Creator, the pain of the chastisement gradually diminishes, the disposition to murmur gently subsides, and the grace of resignation is confirmed in the soul. A provocation received from a fellow-creature tempts us to impatience and anger; but if, under the influence of Christian love, our minds are kept unruffled, and we are enabled to return good for evil, the next circumstance of the kind which occurs to us, is felt in a less degree, the third still less, the fourth scarcely at all. The passive impression becomes more and more evanescent, and, almost imperceptibly to ourselves, the character is formed in us of meekness and forbearance.

It appears indeed to be the design of our heavenly Father, that through this peculiar feature in the law of habit, his children who delight in virtue should be gradually delivered from the tyranny of their evil passions. Temptation frequently repeated, and as frequently resisted, will, in due season, lose both its character and its name. As the active habit of virtue is formed and established, the passive feelings which seduce to vice, are more and more weakened. The vanquished party—with slow and unwilling steps indeed, and with frequent attempts to rally—retreats into inaction, and conquering *grace* takes possession of the field.

SECTION IV.

On Discipline.

In order to form a practical view of the nature of discipline, we may, in the first place, direct our attention to the government of man, over the lower animals—" Thou madest him to have dominion over the works of thy hands; thou hast put all things under his feet; all sheep and oxen, yea, and the beasts of the field; the fowl of the air, and the fish of the sea, and whatsoever passeth through the paths of the seas."*

Divested as we are, in the fall, of that *native* authority over animals, which appears to have formed in Adam one feature of the " image" of God, we still retain the remnants of our power. Not only do we enjoy a license to destroy them for our food, but we bring many of them under our yoke, and apply their powers to our advantage and convenience. For this purpose, we make use of *discipline.*

Let any man watch the process by which the untrained colt is fitted for the use and service

---

* Psalm viii. 6—8.

of his owner. By the enticement of food, the guidance of the rein, the restraint of the bit, the stimulus of the whip, the animal, hitherto accustomed to the most irregular movements, is gradually brought into order. Sometimes also he is yoked to a companion, whose mature and steady motions persuade him by example, or compel him by force, to go forward in the same direction, and to adopt the same paces.

Now this is discipline; the means by which it acts are persuasion and compulsion, gentleness and severity, rewards and punishments, and, above all, example; and the end at which it aims is a total change of *custom*, the annihilation of bad and inconvenient habits, and the forming of good and useful ones. In the case before us, however, it is obvious that discipline does not end with the mere process of education; it is the very essence of the established government to which that process leads. By a continued use of the same means, the bad habits which have been subdued are *kept* in subjection, and the good habits which have been formed are maintained and improved.

As we ascend higher to those various kinds of government which men exercise over their own species, we find that the same principles apply;

discipline is still the same, in its nature, its operation, and its effects.

Let a man visit the children in a nursery—the fire-side circle of a growing family—the school of boys or girls—or the college of young men—and in all these instances he will find, or ought to find, a system of education and government, conducted by discipline. The babes, the growing family, the children at school, and the rising members of the college, are all under training. By persuasion and warning, by gentleness and severity, by rewards and punishments, by alluring to good and deterring from evil, by precept and instruction, and, above all, by the ever-acting force of example, they are severally taught to overcome their bad habits, and to form others which are suitable to their calling and condition. And in each of these cases, the government which is, in the first instance, established by these means, is afterwards conducted and maintained in a similar manner.

When we extend our views to states and nations, we find that the same principles are applicable. Whatsoever may be the form of government which any people adopt, it ought ever to be the object of the legislative and ruling power, to improve the community over which it is placed, in wealth, in civilization, and in moral order. This improvement is indeed the professed object of every government—an object not to be accomplished by any one set of men—but to be pursued through a series of ages and generations. And although it has been hitherto the lot of nations to rise to a certain pitch of prosperity, and afterwards to decline, there can be no doubt, that in any people which should adopt a policy truly conformed to the will of God, there would be a constant progress in prosperity and happiness, and no decay. Even in that imperfect state of things, however, which now exists, every nation may be considered under *training*, as well as under *government;* and, in a large sense of the term, *discipline* is the means by which both these objects are accomplished. The whole system of criminal jurisprudence, a large proportion of civil laws, together with national institutions of a literary or moral nature, constitute a scheme of *discipline.* The means used are restraint and encouragement, instruction and example, punishments and rewards. The end proposed is the subjection of those habits in the community, which interrupt the national welfare, and the formation of others which profit and adorn society.

Such is the nature, and such the operation of discipline, in the various kinds of government which are conducted by men. We may now proceed to take a brief view of the same principles, as they are unfolded in the government of God over mankind.

In His natural government over us (independently of all moral considerations) we are placed under a system of training, and every period of life is intended as a preparation for that which succeeds it. More especially it is the ordinance of our Creator, that during the progress of youth, we should be gradually furnished with those qualifications of body and mind, which fit us for manhood and advancing life.

Every description of voluntary action, bodily or mental, is brought to its maturity by experience and custom, and precisely by the same means do individuals qualify themselves for their peculiar station or calling in society. We have already observed that the functions of the mind, the arts of life, the tempers and dispositions, all of which are of essential importance to our condition in the world—are alike subject to this general rule.

Let us for a moment picture to ourselves a person who should start up in an instant from infancy to maturity, and be a man in the world without any habits at all. What a speechless, senseless, ungovernable creature he would be! The mere impulsive power of body and mind would, on the supposition, be full grown; but how awkward would be his motions, how deluded his sight, how absurd his reasonings, how unrestrained his conduct! How utterly unfit would he be both for the general purposes of life, and for the functions of any peculiar calling!

True indeed it is, that our Creator might have at once bestowed upon us, as he did on our first parents, all our faculties in such a state of mature action, as would have fitted them to every external circumstance, and precluded the necessity of growth and education. But he has seen fit to ordain otherwise. It is one of the most obvious laws of his government over us, that the qualities both of mind and body, which fit us for the world, should, for the most part, be precisely such as are the result of long continued trial and experience.

More especially since we are placed in a state of trial, as it regards even our temporal welfare, it is absolutely necessary for us to form the habit of prudence and self-restraint—to learn to resist the temptations by which we are surrounded *to act unwisely*— to accustom ourselves to abstain from present gratification, in order to insure our future well-being.

Now, for these purposes, our Heavenly Father places us under *discipline*. By furnishing us with incitements to cultivate all our powers; by the force of instruction and example; by crosses and disappointments on the one hand, and encouragement and success on the other; by punishing us for our imprudence, and rewarding us for our self-denial—he affords us an ample scope for subduing every useless or dangerous habit, and for establishing such as will qualify us for our temporal sphere. If we give ourselves up to this discipline, and thus co-operate with the benevolent designs of our Creator, we mostly obtain as great a degree of worldly comfort as properly belongs to our changeable lot. If, on the contrary, we rebel against these divine provisions, and give ourselves over to injurious habits, we are sure to reap an abundant harvest of disquietude and misery.

That these things are true, as it relates to matters of a purely temporal nature, every one must acknowledge; but secondly, under the *moral* government of God, the same principles apply with double force. In the great work of subduing those vicious propensities which are opposed to his will, and of attaining to those virtues which he approves and rewards, the faculty of habit is abundantly brought into play; and this faculty, under divine grace, is redeemed from its corruptions, and directed in the right way, by means of *moral discipline.* If we give way to temptation, and fall into any sinful habit, we increase the disorder of our moral constitution, *and our state of trial becomes more and more unfavourable.* If, on the contrary, we resist temptation, and form, through obedience to the Holy Spirit, the habit of virtuous restraint, our moral constitution is improved, and the dangers to which we are here exposed are gradually lessened.

That some such process is necessary, independently of the consideration of our fallen state, is evident, as Bishop Butler remarks, from the very nature of particular propensities. Since these propensities have certain external objects, since it is a law of our constitution that these objects should excite them, and since the excitement is produced whether it can be lawfully acted on or not, it appears to follow that the very presence of the object must have a tendency—be it ever so slight, yet *some* tendency—to tempt to a breach of the divine law. And no sooner is that law broken than the harmony of the soul is destroyed, and the sinner is separated from his Maker How needful, then, for mankind, even had they continued in their pristine condition, would have been the restraining grace of God, and the *habit* of self-denial!

But our first parents sinned, and lost the image of their Creator; their corrupt condition has descended to their posterity, and moral death has overtaken our species. We are under the dominion of Satan, and through his temptations working on our corrupt hearts, we are ever prone to evil habits. What probability is there, therefore, of our being fitted for any wise or worthy purpose, even as it regards the present life, without the intervention of powerful moral discipline?

For this discipline the successive stages of life afford us ample opportunities; and although multitudes refuse to avail themselves of it, yet those who take the Holy Spirit for their guide, and are therefore on the side of the divine administration, will be sure to find it effectual. The vicissitudes of pleasure and pain, of joy and sorrow, to which they are subject, the encouragements and reproofs which they meet with on their way, the very temptations which they are enabled to overcome, are all calculated to fit them for their proper sphere of moral and religious duty.

On such an application of the moral discipline of God, essentially depend our happiness and true prosperity, even in this world. But how infinitely important does the subject become, when we extend our views to the boundless future? Religion teaches us that, in the world to come, we shall be rewarded or punished according to our conduct here; and also, that the present life is the sole opportunity allotted to us, of *preparation* for eternal bliss. Now and now only, is the time in which we can be converted to God, divested of every evil tendency, confirmed in purity, submission, and charity, and prepared for breathing the element of heaven.

We are, indeed, assured, that many of those graces which we are taught to seek in this world, will no longer be needed there. Our hope will be lost in fruition, our faith in vision, our patience and long-suffering in the fulness of enjoyment. Nevertheless, we have every reason to believe that the state of mind, which can alone fit us for these celestial pleasures, is precisely such as is formed by the exercise, here below, of all these Christian virtues. Under divine mercy and grace, it is, for the most part, the practical result of action, experience, habit, and *moral discipline*.

Before I leave the subject of discipline, I am inclined to particularize a few examples.

Visit the nursery, in which a company of little ones are left to the unrestrained impulse of their wild nature—nothing meets the eye but a scene of disorder; nothing falls upon the ear but dissonant cries of impatience and distress on the one hand and of boisterous pleasure on the other. The voice of the nurse first commanding, next *imploring* better behaviour, dies on the air without producing the smallest effect, and if the mother of the family happens to enter, the utmost stretch of her authority produces only a moment's pause. She is a woman of the world, who thinks little of her domestic duties, and is destitute of all notions of discipline, both in the restraint of herself, and in the government of her children. The consequence is "confusion worse confused," not merely at the present time, but during all the subsequent stages of an unhappy family history.

Enter another nursery, still more populous it may be, where the Christian mother, who has herself submitted to the regulation of divine grace, and knows the secret of the authority of love, is accustomed to exercise her genial and resistless sway. All is contentment, ease and quiet happiness among the children who are capable of speaking and thinking, while even the infant seems charmed into silence. The school-room, in which the same mother, or some able representative, conducts the great affair of early education, presents a spectacle of ready obedience, happy industry, and at least equal enjoyment under a new phase. By what means are these effects produced? By Christian discipline; not without a small measure of severity when required, and the steady maintenance of the rights of government, but characterized throughout by all the tenderness of love and kindness—instruction and example, the meanwhile, going on together hand in hand. What again is the general result? A peaceful stability in the tie between parent and child, during the whole course of their joint lives; an orderly development both of faculty and duty in the growing members of the family; harmony throughout the fire-side circle; and above all, hearts well prepared by parental care and cultivation, for the reception of the grace of God.

It would be difficult to find a more agreeable manifestation of the good effects of discipline, than in a well managed school on the Lancasterian system. There are some five hundred boys in it, as we may suppose; yet when these numerous pupils are seated at their desks on a floor rising as it recedes, they all face their master, whose eye is continually upon them; they all hear his voice, and feel its magic power, when he demands their responses, or hushes them into silence. Monitors are ever at hand to check every rising irregularity, and to entice them onward, in a course of obedience and industry, by the force of example; and when they form their circles for reading or arithmetic, these young professors become the centres of action, and in teaching others, are abundantly taught themselves. Corporal inflictions are banished from the school, and punishment of any kind, after the first stage of discipline, is seldom resorted to. Sufficient is the stimulus of the daily mark, and the half-yearly or quarterly reward. But the true efficacy of the plan, both for the present order and comfort, and for the future well-being of this energetic multitude, depends on the daily infusion of sound, moral and religious principles, and the sure though gradual formation of *good habits.*

Painful must it be to the Christian, to observe the movements and evolutions of a regiment of soldiers—yet not without useful lessons as it regards the power of discipline. How harmonious their steps! how seemly their gait! how unbroken their lines! how skilful their handling of the musket or sword! how swift their obedience to the "winged word" of command! Strange, indeed, is it to compare this living sentient clockwork, with the clumsy appearance and irregular gestures of the raw recruits. Here indeed we see the full effect of imperative sway, perpetual training and teaching, rewards and punishments, and, above all, the ever-present influence of pattern or example. And what is the awful consequence? Reasoning, responsible beings, men destined for immortality, are converted into mere machines, ready to be applied, at a moment's notice, to the butchery and destruction of their fellows.

In prisons, we have to deal with the most corrupt and degraded of our species. Who does not perceive that a commonwealth inflicts a deep wound on its vital interests, when it consigns the criminal part of the community within some vast inclosure, to total idleness and uncontrolled mutual association? Who does not know that the young and inexperienced offender is sure to emerge from such a place of confinement, armed with tenfold terrors for the society to which he belongs? These are evils which all good men must deplore, but which it is not always very easy to remedy. Yet a remedy *may be* found in well-ordered *discipline*. Let our prisons be so constructed as to afford the opportunity of judicious classification and perfect inspection; let every class of our prisoners be under constant superintendence—the men under the care of men, the women under that of officers of their own sex *solely;* let them be carefully watched by night as well as by day; let them never be idle; and let their employment, if possible, be such as to invite to industry, rather than to render it odious and painful. Above all, let them be carefully instructed in the knowledge of true religion, and led by the hand of Christian kindness to the Saviour. *He* can bring them under that divine discipline of the cross, which is the only sure preparation for virtue here, and eternal happiness hereafter.*

---

* I have had many opportunities of observing the working of the two systems of prison discipline, which are now chiefly in vogue. I have watched the *silent* industry of crowded companies in some prisons, and in others have repeatedly visited the solitary cells in which criminals were at work at their respective mechanical arts, and in which they received the visits of their religious instructors. I could have rejoiced in the order of some of the former prisons, had I not marked the depression which dwelt on the countenances of their inmates, and discovered that the grand secret of this order is the ever-present whip. Nor could I conceal from myself that notwithstanding the prevailing silence, connections might easily

He it is undoubtedly from whom emanates all rightful authority for the government of the *church*, and for the *discipline* adopted by any particular society of Christians. In dependence on Christ, our Holy and Omnipresent Head, Christians, when they form themselves into bodies, ought certainly to pay great regard to this part of their privileges and their duty. They ought to be subject one to another in love, and to form such regulations as shall insure the right education and training of their youth, a

---

be formed among the criminals, which could not fail, on their quitting the prison, to endanger society, and enlarge the sphere of crime.

On the whole, I prefer the separate, to the silent system; yet solitary confinement is capable of awful abuse. Be it ever remembered, that it is intolerable to human nature, and utterly unjustifiable for any lengthened period, except when it is accompanied by ample alleviations. These are constant employment, good nourishment, plenty of air and exercise, clear views through the window of each cell, of the sunny or starry heaven, and above all, Christian teaching and superintendence, and the *frequent* visits of the benevolent and good. When we speak of the "*separate* system," we mean the system which *isolates* criminals in confinement, from their *fellow prisoners*. This meaning ought always to be accompanied by the understanding, that these wretched beings are never to be consigned to hopeless solitude, but are to be nurtured, instructed, helped and cherished, by those who will set them a good example, and lead them, by the gentle hand of kindness, into the paths of sobriety, honesty, and peace.

needful care for the support and comfort of their poor members, and an effectual, moral and religious oversight of the body at large. They must not forget the salutary advice of an apostle, " Brethren, if a man be overtaken in a fault, ye which are spiritual restore such an one in the spirit of meekness; considering thyself lest thou also be tempted. Bear ye one another's burdens, and so fulfil the law of Christ."* But while the most experienced and spiritual members of the church are rightly employed in reclaiming the wanderers, and in exercising a just control over the flock, it is the whole society in any particular place, district, or country, in which, under Christ, the power of regulating the conduct of its members, properly resides. Such is the pattern of church government, and of the discipline to which it leads, presented to us in the New Testament. In the meantime " the Spirit divideth to every man severally as he willeth," and as the members of the church are individually careful to submit to his divine influence and authority, the blessed result will be order, harmony, and peace—all will " grow up into Him in all things which is the head, even Christ, from whom the whole body,

---

* Gal. vi. 1, 2.

fitly framed together, and compacted by that which every joint supplieth, according to the effectual working in the measure of every part, maketh increase of the body, to the edifying of itself in love: Eph. iv. 15, 16.

Such are the true principles, and such, through the operation of divine grace, is the happy effect of a well ordered union and *discipline*, in particular Christian societies. But we are never to forget, that the church of Christ upon earth consists of all those of every name and nation (to whatsoever form of administration and church government they may be accustomed) who are truly converted to God, and "baptized by one Spirit into one body." These living ones are scattered over the world under a vast variety of circumstances, and although all united by a hidden tie, are often, in an outward point of view, total strangers one to another. Yet wheresoever the children of the Lord are to be found, and whatsoever the peculiar complexion of their worship, or their creed, they are all, in a high and searching sense of the term, *under discipline*. They know that they are not their own masters, but subject to the yoke of Him who has redeemed them from the slavery of sin and Satan, and has himself an absolute right to rule over them as he pleases. They willingly submit themselves to his government; they are moulded by his plastic hand into the shape and character which he approves; they delight in imitating his example; they shrink from all that can involve them in his wrath; they pant for the glorious reward which he alone can bestow upon them; they take up their cross daily in the midst of an evil and degenerate world, that they may follow him faithfully, in renouncing the world, the flesh, and the evil one. Thus, by a *discipline* ordered and applied in perfect wisdom and love, they are prepared, in the end, to arise above all temporal things, and to rejoice for ever in the presence of their God and Saviour.

CHAPTER II.

ON BAD HABIT.

Had mankind continued upright, and had that faculty of habit, which the Creator has bestowed upon our species, always been applied to its proper ends, the extent of its benefits would have been vast indeed. Certainly, it is only reasonable to believe, that through a long course of self-denial and piety, our outward temperance and inward purity would have become stable as a rock; our love to God and man, a bright and perpetual flame; our perception of his law written on the heart, quick and vivid as lightning, and our obedience to its dictates, swift and uniform like the progress of time. Nor can we doubt that under the control of the law of God, our intellectual powers might gradually have attained to a very high degree of clearness, comprehensiveness, and strength.

These are no idle dreams, but fair deductions from what we know of the nature and operation of the faculty of habit; but alas, "the crown is fallen from our heads; woe unto us, that we have sinned."* A faculty which might have been the means of raising us to the highest pitch of human virtue, and of greatly enlarging our capacities as rational beings, is perverted to contrary ends, and now operates with prodigious strength in a wrong direction—confirming our fallen race in the unlawful indulgence of self, and in rebellion against our Heavenly Father.

The Scriptures fully justify this assertion when they speak of the wicked *ways* of mankind; for the "way" of a man is in his *habit*. Thus we read, that shortly before the flood, " God looked upon the earth, and behold it was corrupt; for all flesh had corrupted his *way* upon the earth."† Again, the Psalmist says—and the Apostle repeats his saying—" There is none righteous, no, not one, there is none that understandeth, there is none that seeketh after God; they are all gone out of the way, they are together become unprofitable; there is none that doeth good, no, not one—destruction and misery are in their *ways*, and the *way* of peace they have not known."‡

---

* Lam. v. 16. † Gen. vi. 12.
‡ Rom. iii. 10—17. Comp. Ps. xiv. 1—3, &c.

In point of fact, Scripture and experience unite in affording a melancholy evidence that mankind, in their fallen nature, are under the dominion of Satan, "the god of this world." Now if any one should inquire what is the main instrument by which he confirms his authority over us—first, gently chaining his slaves, and afterwards, by imperceptible degrees, increasing the weight and number of their fetters—the answer is plain. The instrument which he delights to use for this purpose, is *evil habit*.

In order to make the subject clear, we cannot do better than select an example. Let us examine the history of some notorious criminal who is about to suffer the last penalty of the law. What was the beginning, and what the progress of his "*way?*" Very probably in early life he was induced, under a loose education, to neglect the Sabbath, and to exchange the duties of public worship for amusement and dissipation. Under such circumstances he naturally addicted himself to games of chance, and to this stimulus as naturally added another, that of ardent spirits. While the habits of idleness, gambling, and drinking to excess, were winding themselves around him, his power of self-control was gradually weakened, and his impatience of the control of others grew stronger by indulgence. Gross ideas with which he had become familiar were for ever at hand, like demons waiting on his steps, to conduct him into sin; and the force of this mental association was multiplied tenfold by the example and influence of wicked company. His passions now became ungovernable, and must be satisfied at any cost. The line of integrity was presently broken through; falsehood flowed from his lips as a matter of course, and no longer did he hesitate to seize the property of his neighbour. He sought the midnight hour as a cover for his crimes, and deeds of darkness became first his habit, next his delight. Blasphemy and rebellion against his Maker, confirmed by custom, were soon accompanied by a reckless cruelty towards his fellow-men. Habituated by degrees to rapine and violence, and bound in Satan's adamantine chain, he at length completed his race of wickedness, by a deliberate act of murder.

Every one who examines the moral philosophy of such a case, must perceive that it was through the *faculty of habit*, that sin, small in its beginning, and most insinuating in its progress, obtained its perfect mastery over the mind of the transgressor. The passive impression of virtue gradually declined; the active principle of vice was settled in the constitution. The several bad habits which the individual had formed, all attained to their maturity by an imperceptible growth: and although, perhaps, distinct in their nature, they wrought with a combined force in promoting and completing his ruin.

From an example, in which a number of bad habits are connected together, and operate with nearly equal strength, we may turn to others, in which particular sins are so predominant as to imbue and mark the whole character. How deadly is the condition, how terrible the prospects of the confirmed drunkard, and of the inveterate gamester! In each of them, the corruption of the human heart, common to us all, assumed a peculiar bias, each had his easily besetting sin, his weak spot to which Satan might best address his temptations. Both began their course of sin in a very inconspicuous manner—the water weakly mingled with spirits—the occasional game of chance for a small sum. In each case, however, the growth of the habit, although at first gentle, and almost imperceptible, was sure and steady, and was quickened as it proceeded. The liquor grew stronger and stronger, the draughts from time to time were enlarged and multiplied, the game became habitual instead of occasional, the amount staked was continually on the increase. As the passive impression produced in each case by its appropriate stimulus faded away, the quantity or power of the stimulus itself was, from a sort of sad necessity, augmented; and with every step in the process, the proneness to the sin became more resistless, more constitutional. Now, at length the gamester is prepared to stake his whole remaining fortune on the throw of a die, rather than be deprived of an excitement which has enslaved his very nature; and should the drunkard see before him a glass of ardent spirits, and be assured that the salvation of his soul depended on his abstaining from the draught, the liquor, nevertheless, would, in all probability, be swallowed in a moment.* Such are the small beginnings, the insinuating progress, and the final and perfect triumph of evil habit? Instruction, entreaty, amendment for an hour, a day, a week, are all in vain. "The dog is turned to his own vomit again, and the sow that was washed to her wallowing in the mire."†

Can any thing be more calculated to deprive

---

* Such was the melancholy confession made to a gentleman of my acquaintance by an inveterate gin-drinker.

† 2 Pet. ii. 22.

the soul of all its better powers and loftier hopes, and finally to sink it in the pit of perdition, than habits of sensuality and cruelty? These are sometimes displayed, distinctly from each other, in different characters, but they are often united in the same person. Evidences of this truth are afforded by the history of a Tiberius, a Nero, and a Heliogabalus; and on a still larger scale, in modern times, by the blood-stained records of the slave-trade and slavery. The slave-driver long accustomed to the use of men as cattle, to the arbitrary infliction of terrible punishment, to the public exposure and torture of females, and to the unbridled indulgence of his own lusts, is surely one of the most degraded of his species.

For a time, probably, his heart was affected by the sorrows of the oppressed, and he blushed at the notion of unrestrained licentiousness; but the passive impressions of pity and shame subsided by degrees; the active principles of cruelty and lust took possession of his nature; the wreck of decency became his pleasure, the cries of the wounded, music in his ears! Such a man is surely an object of the deepest compassion; he is the captive of Satan, the slave of bad habit; nothing can rescue him from destruction, but the hand of Omnipotent mercy!

A slave owner in one of the Bahamas was once convicted, together with his wife, of fatally punishing a female slave for some trifling offence, and of rubbing red pepper into the eyes of their dying victim, in order to aggravate her torments.

They were tried and found guilty of the offence, and sentenced to a short imprisonment! But who were the objects of sorrow and compassion in the island, on this horrible occasion? Not the murdered slave—but the imprisoned murderers. On them alone was condolence lavished by their equals in society, and when the time of their confinement had elapsed, they were politely greeted, and publicly entertained. Now every one knows that such scenes would have been impossible in England. Humanity *could not* have been thus outraged, public sympathy *could not* have been thus distorted, except under the influence of a wicked system, confirmed and established by *habit*. The whole circumstance affords a teaching lesson respecting the influence of a faculty, which, when perverted, is capable of blinding the understanding to every moral truth, and of hardening the heart against every impression of mercy.

When it was declared in prophecy to Hazael the Syrian prince, that he would "slay the young men of Israel, dash the children," and perpetrate still more shocking enormities, he answered Elisha, and said—" but what! is thy servant a *dog*, that he should do this great thing?"* That he should ever be guilty of such crimes, might then seem to him beyond the range of possibility; but under the influence of ambition, *habit* wound her chain around him; and man degenerated to the beast, and after a certain lapse of time, the prediction was accomplished. Who has not heard of the Roman Emperor who began his career of cruelty, by tormenting flies, in his infancy, and who, as he advanced in life, became, by slow degrees, one of the greatest monsters the world ever saw?

Among the bad and sinful habits which lay waste the happiness of mankind, *war* stands pre-eminent. This is a habit which infests communities as well as individuals, it is to be traced to the evil passions which are common to our species, and it is nurtured by false and dangerous principles in general education. But for the guilt of this prevailing custom, no persons are so deeply responsible as the statesman in the closet and the monarch in the field. Who can read

---

* 2 Kings viii. 12, 13.

the history of Napoleon, without perceiving that in the midst of all his glory, he was the mere slave of his own passions, and of a destructive and terrible custom? Nursed and tutored in arms—an embryo general and conqueror at school—introduced, in early life, to an arena of fierce contention—entrusted with armies before years and experience had made him sober, and intoxicated with early and splendid success, most naturally did he go on from adventure to adventure, and from conquest to conquest. The passive feeling of the terrors of warfare, and of regard for the sufferings of others, faded and vanished. The active propensities of ambition and aggression were wrought into his constitution; and what was the practical result? The wasting of nations, and the sacrifice of millions of human lives! How strange a proof is it of the power of *evil habit*, that murder on this enormous scale should become familiar to the minds of men, that it should be justified on the plea of honour, that it should even be accounted as the height of human glory.

Bad habits of action are, for the most part, inseparably connected with a disordered or vicious state of mind; the disposition prompts the action, and the action confirms the disposition, which becoming at length habitual and constitutional, is like an ever-flowing fountain within us — a fountain of *bitter* waters.

Some persons are prone to view almost every subject through a ridiculous medium; it is their pleasure and their genius to discover odd associations, and there is nothing so familiar on the one hand, or so grave on the other, as not to excite their faculty of jesting. It is surprising in how great a degree this faculty is strengthened by indulgence, and how quickly it becomes the leading feature of a man's manners and character. When this is the case, it is easy to perceive the truth of the Apostle's declaration, that jesting is not " convenient ;" by which term he may be understood to mean, that it is unsuitable to the purposes of life, and inconsistent with the dignity of the Christian character. The inveterate jester is sure to lose his weight in society, the wares in which he deals are contemptible, and when he sets his wanton foot on sacred ground, and learns to deride the doctrines of religion, or to joke in the words of Scripture, his habit becomes a perilous one indeed. Who shall say that such a man is not in danger of laughing away his soul into endless woe?

A notorious infidel of modern times, was in

his *earlier days* reputed to be a religious man, and was even engaged in the ministry of the gospel. Two features in his character (as I learn from a person who knew him well) combined to lead him astray, and were finally the means of *changing* him into a blasphemer against God. The first was self-conceit; the second was a resistless habit of turning every thing into ridicule.

Antiquity had her weeping, as well as her laughing philosopher, and there are *murmurers* in the world as well as *jesters*. Some persons are prone to a sour temper, and habituated to gloomy views. It is not that they have that lively impression of their own unworthiness and of the sinfulness of the world, which leads them to embrace and promote the gospel. It is that they lament over their lot, perceive only the dark side of the question, and take a distorted view both of themselves and others. Such a state of mind is fixed and matured through a long course of querulous emotions, and these are perpetually strengthened by ebullitions of temper and complaining words. The habit of the murmurer is indeed an evil one; it is utterly opposed to the gracious designs of our Heavenly Father, who plans our happiness and demands our gratitude and praise. Such a man is exposed to the deepest danger; he may easily go on from bad to worse, until complaint shall become blasphemy—and his awful end may be to "*curse God and die.*"

Still more common is a splenetic humour towards our friends and acquaintances, often productive of sayings not the less cruel because they are witty, and displaying itself, when all wit is wanting, in low-born detraction. This is a humour which, with the sinister practices resulting from it, is ever found to own the sway of habit; and when it is once fixed in the mental constitution, the misanthrope becomes at once miserable himself, and a fruitful source of misery to all around him.

Who cannot trace the influence of custom, in the anxious thoughts, and studious penury of the miser, who, grown rich by slow degrees, starves himself and his dependants, in the same progressive ratio, from an ever-increasing terror of poverty?

"What shall be given unto thee, or what shall be done unto thee, thou false tongue? Sharp arrows of the mighty, with coals of juniper;" Ps. cxx. 4. There is nothing more natural to man than this false tongue; it is inherent in his fallen nature, and is set in action by *him* who was a liar from the beginning, and " the father of it:" John viii. 44. Yet its flippant facility —first in paring down, or exaggerating truth, and at length in sacrificing and demolishing it, without reserve, and on all sorts of occasions— displays in a remarkable manner the insinuating influence, and in the end, irrevocable tyranny of bad habit.

Among the evil customs of mind which infect mankind, may be reckoned those of believing *too much*, and of believing *too little*. Both of them are fraught with danger; the one leads to superstition, the other to atheism.

In the history of idolatry, we find an example, on a most extensive scale, of the *habit* of credulity. Nothing at first sight can be more surprising than the fact that a vast proportion of mankind, both in ancient and modern times, have steadily maintained the practice of adoring images of wood and stone, and have appeared to be destitute of any spring of reason or good sense in themselves, by which they could escape from the bondage of so gross a delusion. Well might the prophet say of the idolater, " a deceived heart hath turned him aside, that he cannot deliver his soul, nor say, is there not a lie in my right hand?"* The main cause of these delusions, is doubtless to be found in that corruption of the heart, which leads men to change "the truth of God into a lie," and to worship and serve the "creature more than the Creator."† But the peculiar faculty of the mind, which Satan perverts in order to this end, is that of habit. The idolater believes that graven images are proper objects of worship, not because there is any show of reason in such a notion, for it is contrary to all reason; but because he has been nurtured in it from his youth, and has been so long accustomed to act on the lie, *as if it were true*, that the belief of it, in spite of reason and evidence, is become almost insuperable. It is wrought up in his constitution, and forms a part of his very nature.

May not an example of the same class be found among professing Christians, in the settled conviction entertained by multitudes, and even by a long series of generations, that the "elements" in the eucharist, when consecrated by a priest, truly become the flesh and blood of Jesus Christ? That when our Lord distributed the bread and wine to his twelve disciples, his body was in dif-

---

* Isaiah xliv. 20.   † Rom. i. 25.

ferent places, and in different states (whole and broken) at the same time, and that now, while glorified in heaven, it is eaten on earth, and eaten in thousands of places at once, appear to me to be propositions which no rational being can be required to believe. Such imaginary facts are not to be mistaken for miracles. The latter have always been proved by the testimony of the senses; they are opposed only to the *order of nature*, and are at all times possible to nature's Author. The former are at variance with the *eternal nature of things;* and no evidence whatsoever, which can be adduced in their favour, can equal the evidence which they contain within themselves, of their own falsehood. They are not, like the great doctrines of Christianity, simply *beyond* reason; they are *contrary* to it, and disprove themselves. That the sun should stand still in its course (or rather the earth be stayed in its rotation) was a miracle. That either the sun or the earth, or any other material substance, should exist in two places at the same moment, is an impossibility. And yet, in spite of this obvious distinction, the doctrine of transubstantiation has become so familiar to thousands of sincere persons, and in some cases to men of superior parts, that they believe in its truth, as fully and implicitly.

as in that of their own existence. What can account for this strange fact, but the all-pervading influence of *habit?*

Nor is the habit of believing too much—of believing *against* reason and *beyond* the limits of truth—one of a harmless and indifferent nature. Superstition is as powerful an enemy against virtue and happiness, as has ever been let loose upon mankind by " the Prince of the power of the air." Who does not know that the annals of heathenism are disfigured by all that is licentious, and stained by all that is bloody ? Among those who profess Christianity, superstition is, for the most part, inseparably connected with bigotry and intolerance; and who can deny that additions made to the divine fabric on merely human authority, are sure to mar its beauty, and diminish its strength ?

Christianity is, in its nature, *reasonable.* Its truth is proved to the satisfaction of every fair inquirer, by miracles performed and attested, by prophecies fulfilled, and above all, by the experience of true believers in the Son of God. Some of those essential doctrines on which its whole system is founded, are indeed far above the reach of the natural understanding of man; they relate to those secrets of an infinite Being, which would have been for ever unknown, had they not been revealed; and now that they are revealed, they can be rightly understood and estimated only by the humble mind, and under the influence of the Holy Spirit. Yet there is not one of these doctrines which is contrary to reason, or which has even the slightest tendency to disprove itself—not one which, when accepted with simplicity, does not bear upon the mind with that native force, which belongs only to *truth*.

How is it then that so many persons fail to appreciate the evidence on which Christianity is founded, and that others, while they confess its divine origin, reject its most important and fundamental parts? These evils must certainly be traced to the pride of the heart of man, to his natural love of darkness, and to that self-righteousness which lulls us to sleep as if we needed not a Saviour. The immediate cause of them, however, is *the habit of believing too little.* " Make the heart of this people fat, and make their ears heavy, and shut their eyes, lest they see with their eyes and hear with their ears, and understand with their heart, and convert and be healed!"*
The Jews were given over to infidelity as a

---

* Isaiah vi. 10.

punishment for their sins; in other words, that grace was withdrawn from them, by which alone their *habitual* incredulity could be overcome. So long had they been accustomed to distrust God, and to place their dependence on a system of their own, that when Jesus came to contradict and overturn it, they "*could* not believe" in their lowly Redeemer. The purity of his doctrine, and the greatness of his miracles, were alike disregarded—evidence, the clearest and the strongest, passed for nothing!

The habit of leaning to our own understanding in matters of religion, and of rejecting every truth which does not accord with our preconceived notions, is one of the most insinuating and dangerous to which we are liable. It soon triumphs, not merely over simple faith, but even over sound evidence, and enlightened reason. Finally, if indulged in, it may conduct the unbeliever downwards, from step to step, in the road of darkness, until "the fool shall say in his heart, there is no God."*

Infidelity, however, even when it fails to blind the understanding, may nevertheless infect the heart. This is indeed its birthplace, and con-

---

* Psalm xiv. 1.

tinues to be its abode, in men of all descriptions and characters, until it is dislodged by grace. What is ungodliness, but *practical* atheism? And must we not allow that while there are many bad habits which peculiarly infest individuals or classes of men, the habit of ungodliness is *universal* in our fallen race? We are by nature the "children of wrath," separated from God by our sins, and while we continue in this state of alienation, we forget and disregard him; we do not live in his fear; we hide ourselves from the light of his law; we have no pleasure in serving him; we are not actuated by *love* towards him; we do not seek his glory. The *impression* of his presence and holiness is always growing weaker; the practice of distrusting and disobeying him, is continually gaining ground upon us; again and again our disaffection breaks out into rebellion, and our natural alienation from the Author of our being, becomes inveterate by *habit*. To this melancholy condition so general among unregenerate men, the doctrine of the prophet applies in all its force. "*Can the Ethiopian change his skin, or the leopard his spots? then may ye also do good that are accustomed to do evil.*"*

---

* Jer. xiii. 23.

Such is the language of experience—of true moral philosophy—of revealed religion. Man, prone to corruption, and inured from his youth to many an evil way, is utterly destitute of any natural or inherent power to save or *change* himself. It is only by the free grace of God that we are enabled to "put off the old man which is corrupt according to the deceitful lusts, and to put on the new man, which after God is created in righteousness and true holiness."*

Nothing indeed can more strongly show the necessity of a divine influence for the regeneration of mankind, than a just view of our present subject. When it is our lot to contend not merely with the original perversion of our nature, but with that state of confirmed corruption and rebellion against the Lord, which is the result of evil *custom*, we may rest assured that in order to overcome these enemies, we stand in absolute need of the power of the Holy Spirit. Without the gracious aid of an Omnipotent and most merciful Being, it is utterly impossible for us to obtain the victory.

Here, however, we must not lose sight of an important distinction. There is a morality, which

---

* Eph. iv. 22—24.

is not *holiness*, and there may also be a change for the better in our moral habits, which is not *sanctification*. We may easily suppose the case of a drunkard, who is convinced of the folly and danger of his course, and is weary of the distress entailed on himself and his family by his intemperate habits. Urged by no mean motives, he makes a strong effort to escape from his trammels; he places himself, perhaps, under the care of a friend, joins a Temperance Society, and finally, while he continues to abstain from all intoxicating drinks, he gradually loses his propensity, and becomes a sober man. Now, if the external reform has been effected without the surrender of his heart to God, it must not be hailed as a work of saving grace.

On a similar principle, it cannot be denied that a certain degree of proficiency in good moral habits—for example, in beneficence, industry, honest dealing, and self-government—is sometimes attained by persons who appear to have but little true godliness; and it is possible that in consequence of careful training, their children, after them, may maintain the practice of the same virtues. Much more clearly, however, among children who are brought up by religious parents, in a knowledge of the Scriptures, and in the nurture and admonition of the Lord, we often perceive the operation of a conscientious principle, long before we have reason to conclude that they are " born of the Spirit." Nor can it be doubted, that the Christian parent is often successful in weaning his offspring from bad habits of thought and action, and in leading them forward, from one step to another, in the path of virtue.

In all these cases much is to be ascribed, in my opinion, to a divine influence. God is on the side of virtue, and he may condescend to bless an honest effort directed to virtuous ends, even in those who are not yet his children by adoption. With regard to the offspring of religious parents, there can be no doubt that *every degree* of success in the work of Christian education, must be attributed to His blessing. The *preparatory* work of the Spirit has evidently a vast scope in the divine economy, and who shall venture to affix a limit to the secret yet manifold visitations of *light from above?*

Nevertheless, as long as the soul of man continues in its unregenerate state, it will be sure to harbour many evil habits, and above all others, the habit of *ungodliness*. Nothing short of an absolute change of heart—a new birth unto righteousness—can cure the evil at its root;

nothing less powerful than saving grace can lead to sanctification, that is, to the *formation of the habit of holiness.*

Now as grace is absolutely necessary for this highest of moral purposes, so is it adequate to its end. This is a truth which we cannot fail to deduce from the Omnipotence of God, and it is confirmed both by Scripture and experience. Scripture assures us that " the fruit of the Spirit is in all goodness, and righteousness, and truth,"[*] and experience affords abundant proofs, that the living and abiding faith of the humble Christian, is productive of a sober, righteous, and godly life. The believer in Jesus is indeed engaged in an arduous warfare, and long must he expect to contend with indwelling sin and *evil habit*, before he obtains his final victory. Nevertheless he has God on his side, and by means of a power infinitely superior to his own, he is enabled to forsake the works of darkness, and to walk watchfully before the Lord, in the light of the living.

Far be it from me to undervalue the habits of virtue by whomsoever practised, and in whatsoever form. Unquestionably they *have* their value— they also *have* their reward—even when they

---

[*] Eph. v. 9.

appear to be the mere result of system and education. But the morality produced by vital religion is of a far superior character; no earthly, spurious article—no outward show, without intrinsic worth. The soil from which it springs, is a broken heart, the element in which it flourishes, is the *love of God*, and the end to which it leads, is a state of perfect and endless purity.

> "Struck by that light, the human heart,
> A barren soil no more,
> Sends the sweet smell of grace abroad,
> Where serpents lurked before.
>
> "The soul, a dreary province once
> Of Satan's dark domain,
> Feels a new empire formed within,
> And owns a heavenly reign."

To prescribe bounds, in our own wisdom, to the influence of that Spirit, which, like the wind, bloweth where it listeth, and to assert that grace cannot operate where Christianity is unknown— would ill become creatures so blind and ignorant as we are. Yet, beyond all question, the gospel of our Lord Jesus Christ is the great *instrument* which God has appointed for turning away mankind from their iniquities, and for leading them into "newness of life." It is the *principal means* employed by the Holy Spirit for delivering us from our natural corruption, and for changing our bad habits into good ones.

That Christianity is, with a perfect wisdom and skill, adapted to the great work of renovating mankind, those will be the most ready to allow, who have the most experimental acquaintance with its nature and structure. Revealed religion detects our corruption, unfolds the heart-searching spirituality of the law, makes known the terrors and joys of an eternal future, displays the free mercy of God in Christ Jesus, and offers to all that are athirst, the waters of eternal life. Thus does it bring into play the *purest and most powerful motives* by which a rational creature can be actuated, and bears, with an unrivalled force, on the mind and heart of man.

The terrors of the law, the holiness of God the doctrine of man's responsibility, and the revelation of judgment to come, all unite in exciting an awful *fear*. The experience of divine grace, the earnest of the Spirit, the promise of heaven, are equally adapted to raise our *hope*. These two motives are each of deep importance in the work of religion; the one leads to watchfulness and circumspection; the other animates our efforts and inspires our courage in the Christian race. But above all, *love* is a motive of sovereign efficacy, and it is brought into full action by the gospel, and the gospel only. By the glad tidings of the love and mercy of our Creator, in Christ Jesus, the Christian is taught to love God in return. "The *love of Christ* constraineth us"—this is the mainspring of the *devotion of the heart* to God. Love demands an unconditional surrender of our wills to the will of our Heavenly Father; it binds us by the dearest of ties to the service of our Redeemer. And not only does this best and strongest of motives lead to decision in religion, but it imbues the Christian with the principle of *perseverance.* It imparts to him a perpetual movement of spirit towards the supreme object of his affections, towards the heaven in which He dwells, and towards the holiness without which no man can see him.

Were it proposed to raise to the top of a lofty hill some vast and ponderous substance lying at its base, how vain for that purpose would be the unassisted efforts of the human arm! But apply the lever and the pulley, each in its own place, and according to its respective action, and the difficulty, which appeared to be insuperable, is rapidly overcome. In spite of every obstruction, the mighty mass moves upwards, its course is gradual but certain, and presently it rests on the summit—the victory is won. Very similar is the work of true religion. The human heart is a dead weight, buried in miry clay, chained to the pit of corruption by the force of evil habit. And there is no native power inherent in man, by which he can deliver it from its debased condition, or raise it towards those heavenly regions where all is godliness, purity, and peace. But when, through the matchless influence of Christianity, our motives are set to work—when fear operates on the soul from one side, and hope from the other; above all, when it is raised and impelled from below, by the constraining and elevating force of love — it cannot fail to move in a heavenly direction. Lightened and purified as it ascends, it is sure, in the end, to be made victorious, and to find its resting place on Mount Zion, "the city of the great King." Yet we know that the mechanical forces will be utterly useless unless there be applied an external power to bring them to bear. We still require the human arm, or the strength of the horse, the falling water, or the rising steam. And just as useless will be our very best motives for effecting that triumph over self, which is the main purpose of Christianity, unless they are quickened into action, and rightly directed and applied, by the immediate influences of the Holy Spirit.

It appears then, that had mankind continued in their state of pristine innocence, the faculty of habit might have been productive, in our species, of an indefinite degree both of virtue and power; but that under the fall, it is the means by which our natural depravity is confirmed, and the bonds of Satan multiplied and strengthened, in a fearful manner. The subject has been illustrated by the case of the desperate felon—of the gamester and the drunkard—of the sensual and the cruel—of the warrior and conqueror—of the confirmed jester—of the murmurer against God —of the misanthrope and the liar—of him who believes too much — of him who believes too little—and finally by a view of a bad habit universal among unregenerate men, that of *ungodliness*. The effect of merely human efforts in correcting bad habits, and in the pursuit of virtue, and especially the practical result of a guarded education, have been duly appreciated; but we have clearly seen that for a radical cure— for such a change of habit as will fit us for the element of heaven—divine and saving grace is absolutely essential. And lastly, as this grace is essential, so it is sufficient; and the gospel of

Jesus Christ considered, as the instrument, is adapted to its end, with a perfect precision. Its very structure imparts to it, under the Spirit of God, a matchless influence over the dispositions, the feelings, and the conduct of men. It is the best of weapons for slaying our evil habits, for cleaving our chains asunder, and for delivering us from all our corruptions.

In conclusion, however, we have to offer one practical remark. Although the regeneration and redemption of man, is exclusively *a work of grace*, we are commanded by the divine precepts, and enabled by the divine Spirit, to co-operate with the Lord for the accomplishment of this blessed purpose. "*Work out your own salvation* with fear and trembling, for it is God *who worketh in you* to will and to do of his good pleasure."* Our warmest desires, our most strenuous efforts, our watchfulness and prayers, our undivided mind, must all be thrown into the work. We must carry on a perpetual warfare with all our evil habits, we must check and counteract them severally, by forming *opposite habits* on the side of virtue. In dependence on the great Captain of our salvation, we must rally

---

* Phil. ii. 12.

our own forces together, and *oppose a friend to a foe in every part of the line of battle.* We must never cast away a single article of the Christian's armour. Availing ourselves, from day to day, of that divine influence which is so freely bestowed upon us, we must triumph over the passive impressions which temptation produces, by means of the ever-acting, ever-growing principles of faith and obedience.

CHAPTER III.

ON GOOD HABIT.

SECTION I.

General Principles of Education.

We have already found occasion to observe, that among the lower animals, *instinct* is the prevailing characteristic. The crocodile seeks the water as soon as he bursts from his shell; the new-born lizard, or worm, or fly, is presently invested with the ancient habits of his race; the birds of passage require no tutelage to enable them to choose the right time for their migration; the bee of this day's generation is just as skilful a builder, and just as wise a geometrician, as his sire or his grandsire. All these are led along in their appointed path by a ruling faculty which requires no training, because it is susceptible of no improvement.

Yet the constitution, even of dumb animals, affords a certain scope for the formation of habit, and therefore for discipline and education — a scope which (as we have already remarked) is greatly enlarged when they come under the dominion of man, and are subject to domestication.

On the other hand, with man himself, although he practises a few instinctive actions, education is of paramount importance. The government of God over him, both natural and moral, is distinguished by nothing more clearly than by a system of training, and the faculty of habit is the medium through which this system is carried into effect. That passive impressions should be weakened, and active principles strengthened, by repetition, and that every kind of action should become easy to us in proportion to the frequency with which it is performed, are laws of our nature which serve a vast variety of ends. Some of these ends may be far beyond the reach of our present knowledge or conception, and there can be no greater presumption on our parts, than to pretend to limit the *final causes* for which God ordains and acts. Yet we run no risk in asserting that one obvious purpose of this divine economy is, that by the right use of all our faculties in the days of our youth, we may be prepared for the functions and duties of mature life. In like manner, through the performance of these functions and duties, and the consequent settlement in us of certain dispositions and principles, we may, in the meridian of our day, be gradually educated for an honourable and tranquil old age.

When, however, we speak of education as of such essential importance to the destinies of mankind, we by no means confine our views to human parents, teachers, or rulers. The all-wise Creator of man condescends to educate him for the various purposes of his being, and although, to a certain extent, he carries on the work in us through the government and instruction of our fellow-men, yet *they* are nothing more than his instruments.

God has, himself, placed us in circumstances which produce the development of our bodily and mental powers. By an almost infinite variety of excitement, by the guidance of an ever-plastic hand, he invites and even constrains us to use these powers, and by use, to improve and enlarge them. At the same time, he wisely subjects us to discipline and restraint, and by that which we suffer, teaches us what we are to avoid. While he endues us with appetites, and places us in the midst of those objects by which they may be gratified, he inflicts upon us, even here, a variety of punishments for indulging them unduly. By evidence of a practical nature, he proves to us that prudence and self-denial are absolutely essential to our welfare in the world. Above all, however, he commits all our faculties to the rule of conscience; and as a guide to our conscience, enlightens us with his Spirit, and writes his law on the tablet of the heart.

As an example of the education to which we are subjected under the natural government of God, we may again refer to the power, so gradually obtained, in very early life, of correct and intelligent *sight*. He who formed the machinery of the eye—the pupil by which it receives the rays of light, the lenses by which it refracts them, the muscles by which it is directed, and the nerve through which it perceives—prepares the organ for its right use, by an unfelt, yet systematic, schooling. Through the joint application of the other senses, and through the progressive exercise of judgment, the child is taught, by insensible degrees, to see things as they really are, to measure and compare their distances, to understand their true proportions.

It is said that when a young German, who had been confined from his earliest years in a dark dungeon, was transferred to a light apartment, he learned to see aright only by degrees. It was long before he could be made to comprehend that a fine prospect, visible from his window, was any thing more than a confused mass of colours dashed on the shutter. But under a process of education, and when the exercise of his judgment had become habitual, the apparent chaos was brought into order, the several objects of vision were seen in their true places and proportions, and all was harmony and beauty.

Under the training which a good Providence has ordained for us, something of the same kind takes place, though we scarcely know how, with respect to most of our faculties, both of body and mind. By a natural scheme of education and discipline, we are gradually instructed in the proper use of them, and almost in spite of ourselves, they are enlarged and improved as we advance in life. With respect to the faculty by which we judge of right and wrong, there can be no doubt that it is miserably weakened in fallen man, and that it is liable to be greatly perverted by education and example. Nevertheless, the law of the LORD can never change; and the influence of the Holy Spirit, when it is submitted to, will restore this highest of our faculties to its original order; it will stamp upon its decisions the unvarying features of holiness and truth.

We may now proceed to consider, what are the right principles of education, regarded as the work of *man?*

The first principle which ought ever to be kept in view by parents, tutors, and rulers of every description is, *that they are mere instruments in the hands of the Creator,* and that it is at once their bounden duty and highest wisdom, to act in the character of his vicegerents, and in conformity to his will. This principle lies at the root of the science of education, and unless it be laid down clearly in the first instance by those to whom is committed the training of young people, and steadily maintained during the whole process of their work, they will be sure to involve themselves in irremediable error, and to plunge the objects of their care into darkness and sorrow.

On this first principle depend a variety of general rules. Independently of the light of Holy Scripture, nature herself affords us many evidences of that which her Divine Author wills, respecting our bodily and mental functions. The *tendencies* of his natural government over us are often so clear as not to be mistaken; those of his moral government are also discoverable, both from his law written on the heart, and from the perceptible course of his providence. Now, in conducting the work of education, we must endeavour to conform ourselves to these tendencies—we must be co-workers with the Lord; for it is He who made us and governs us, for a purpose of our highest happiness and his own glory.

The following general rules of education may, without difficulty, be deduced from what we perceive and know of the natural and moral government of God. They are rules which the parent or teacher who desires, in the work of education, to co-operate with *His* all-wise design, will by no means venture to disregard or infringe.

I. It is a conspicuous fact that the formation of *good habits*, is one principal means which God has ordained for our being trained to a life of usefulness and happiness. This therefore is a point to which, in every department of education, our attention must be studiously directed; for unless good habits be formed in our children and pupils, it will be all in vain to give them rules. The oftener any rule or precept is repeated, the less is the effect which, on each successive occasion, it will produce on the mind—this decay of the passive impression, can be counteracted only by the habitual exercise of active principles.

Here however it ought to be remarked, that good habits are most easily formed when they anticipate bad ones—*prevention is better than cure.*

II. The faculties with which the Creator has endowed us, both bodily and mental, are made for use, and by means of use, are destined for *improvement.* This is the obvious tendency of nature, and were it not for the obstructions which are perpetually arising from our present imperfect and corrupt condition, it seems probable that the uniform result of youth, would be a perfect condition of all our faculties in maturity. It is the duty of the educator to work in unison with this tendency, to remove the obstructions by which it is hindered, and as far as possible to carry it into effect. We are always to remember that it is the benevolent purpose of Him whom, as guardians of the young, we represent, that the creature under our care should *be made the most of,* both in body and mind.

III. God, in whom dwells the perfection of mind, is *Omniscient;* with his infinite power and wisdom, corresponds the absolute universality of his knowledge. Beyond all doubt it is his gracious design, that our rational minds, which may be compared to a spark from the divine intelligence, should be furnished with knowledge, in proportion to their capacity. To impart knowledge, therefore, to the young, and still more, to adapt their mental faculties to the future and permanent acquirement of it, is a very main concern in the work of education. It is our unquestionable duty, in both these respects, to aim at as high a standard as circumstances will admit.

IV. Yet there is nothing in the course of nature which appears to warrant an excess of cultivation. On the contrary, such an excess is sure to be punished in the end, by the lessening of the very powers which we desire to enlarge. It is evidently the will of the Creator and Ruler of nature, that none of his living creatures should be overstrained. Rest, facility, comfort, and the leisurely play of the faculties, form an indulgent part of our Heavenly Father's training, which the human parent and tutor ought never to forget.

V. To every stage of childhood and youth, there ought to be appropriated its own measure of discipline and instruction. If the work of the instructor does not keep pace with the natural growth of the powers, those powers will never be properly developed; but if it outruns that growth, they will flourish only to wither, they will soon be stunted and decay.*

VI. If God has bestowed upon a child some particular genius, it seems to be the right part of the educator to suffer that genius to answer its purpose, and to work in the same direction. To thwart and contradict it, would be to oppose divine providence, and to mutilate the mental constitution of the child.† Yet he who, in his

---

* "Nec sum adeo ætatum imprudens, ut instantum teneris protinus acerbe putem, exigendamque plenam operam." "*Nor am I so little observant of the years of children as to think that we ought to press severely on those of a tender age, and exact full labour from them:*" Quintilian de Institutione oratoria, lib. i. "Nam ut vascula oris angusti superfusam humoris copiam respuunt; sensim autem influentibus, vel etiam instillatis complentur; sic animi puerorum, quantum excipere possint, videndum est; nam majora intellectu, velut parum apertos ad percipiendum, animos non subibunt." "*For as vessels with narrow mouths reject an abundance of water, when it is poured over them, but are filled with the fluid, when it flows or is dropped into them, by degrees; so must we watch how much the minds of children are able to receive. Things above their understanding will find no entrance into their minds, which are not open to apprehend them:*" Idem, lib. i. 2.

† "Illud tamen in primis testandum est, nihil præcepta atque artes valere nisi adjuvante natura." "*This I must in the first place testify, that our precepts and arts are of no use at all, unless we have nature on our side.*" Quintilian de Instit. orat. Proæm. "Virtus præceptoris haberi solet, nec immerito, dili-

wisdom, bestows the natural taste and genius, provides a variety of checks, by which they may be kept within due bounds. The educator ought to observe these checks, and never suffer a particular bias so to prevail, as to weaken the requisite operation of other faculties; much less to overflow any moral boundary.

VII. All the faculties with which man is endued, are obviously intended to be exerted in harmony with each other, and this harmony depends on subordination. In point of authority, one part of them is set above another. It is the evident design of the Creator, that the powers of the body should be subjected to those of the mind, and be employed under the guidance of reason; and again, both our bodily and intellectual powers are placed under the dominion of conscience. It is one of the first duties of the parent or tutor, to establish and maintain this

---

genter in iis quos erudiendos susceperit, notare discrimina ingeniorum, et quo quemque natura maxime ferat, scire. Nam est in hoc incredibilis quædam varietas, nec pauciores animorum pene, quam corporum formæ." "*It is deservedly considered meritorious in a preceptor, to mark the differences of genius, in those whom he has undertaken to educate, and to ascertain in what direction nature would carry each of them. For there is in this respect an incredible variety, the forms of minds being almost as multifarious as those of bodies:*" Idem, lib. ii. 8.

order, in those who are placed under his care. The least deviation from it will discompose and injure the whole creature.

VIII. Rewards and punishments form a conspicuous part of that training of man, which is carried on by the moral Governor of the universe. It is evident therefore that they are both of them, on proper occasions, legitimate means of discipline, in human education. But God's chief rewarder and punisher, in the present life, is conscience; and the parent or tutor will find all other rewards and punishments comparatively needless, if the *consciences* of the young be watched and cultivated, and preserved in a proper state of tenderness and energy.*

---

* Punishment ought always to be applied with peculiar caution—the motive of fear being much less adapted to some children than to others : " Quosdam continet metus, quosdam debilitat." "*Fear restrains some children, but weakens others :*" Quintil. lib. i. 3. This sagacious writer entertained views on the subject of corporal punishment, which were far beyond the age in which he lived, and would do credit to the 19th century. " Cædi vero discentes, quanquam et receptum sit, et Chrysippus non improbet, minime velim ; primum quia deforme atque servile est, et certe, quod convenit, si ætatem mutes, injuria ; deinde quod si cui tam est mens illiberalis, ut objurgatione non corrigatur, is etiam ad plagas, ut pessima quæque mancipia, durabitur; postremo, quod ne opus erit quidem hac castigatione, si assiduus studiorum exactor adstiterit." " *But I would by no means allow scholars to be beaten, although it is a received practice, and Chrysippus does not disapprove it ; first because it*

This rule however requires a little addition. God has ordained that the decisions of conscience should often be strengthened by the *verdict* of our fellow-men. He has given us a nature which seeks their approbation, and shrinks from their reproofs. Hence we may learn that commendation and blame judiciously administered, are perfectly consistent with the will of our Heavenly Father, and fill a highly important place in the work of education.*

Most of the rules now mentioned will be found, in practice, to have a close dependence on the first, which enjoins the *formation of good habits*. It is chiefly through a right application

---

is a shameful and servile practice—so much so, that if the age be changed, it becomes an injury in law; secondly, because if a lad be of so ignoble a mind as not to be corrected by reproof, he will, like the worst slaves, be hardened even against stripes; lastly, because there will be no need of punishment, if a master be present, who diligently attends to the studies of his pupils;" Idem, lib. i. 3.

* Blame, like punishment, must be sparingly used. Quintilian has marked the danger of it, in matters of learning. "Ne illud quidem admoneamus indigrum est, ingenia puerorum nimia interim emendationis severitate deficere; nam et desperant, et dolent, et novissime oderunt, et quod maxime nocet, dum omnia timent nihil conantur." "*It is not unworthy of our notice, that the abilities of children are apt to fail them, when we too severely criticise their performances; for they despair, and are grieved, and at last hate us; and what is still worse, while they fear every thing they attempt nothing:*" Idem, lib. ii. 4.

of the faculty of *habit*, that the young person is taught to make the most of all his powers; to acquire and store up knowledge; to adapt his exertions to the age and condition of his powers; to pursue his natural genius with diligence, yet within right bounds; and lastly, through divine aid, to submit his body to the government of reason, and both his body and mind to that of conscience. Now it is notorious that the habits of young people are, to a great extent, formed on the model of those examples, with which they are most familiar. And what example is more constantly before their eyes, than that of the parent or tutor who is daily and hourly engaged in educating them?

The effect of example in education, may be illustrated by a reference to the arts of reading and writing. The hand-writing of the pupil is, indeed, assisted by the precepts of his master; but it is *formed* on the copies which his master sets him. The modulations of a young person's voice in reading, may be partly the result of rules laid down for him; but the imitative faculty is here our chief resource—the pupil is sure to read *after the manner* of his teacher. The same principles apply to every branch of education, and exercise a powerful sway over the intellect, the affections and even the moral conduct. Who then can doubt the importance of the following rule?

IX. The educator of youth must place his dependence more upon example than precept. As far as the difference of age will permit, he ought to be a model to his pupils, and lead the way for them not only in forming habits of art, but in the whole process of intellectual, moral, and religious cultivation.* Of this rule, however, there is a second branch of equal importance with the first. While we humbly endeavour to promote the welfare of our children by setting them a good example, we must watch over them as members of *society*, and exercise continual vigilance, that our efforts may not be counteracted by the bad example of other persons, or one of another; for it is a certain truth that "evil communications corrupt good manners." In order to succeed in this endeavour, nothing is more necessary than constant Christian *superintendence*.

* " Frequens imitatio transit in mores." "*Frequent imitation passes into the habits:*" Quintil. lib. i. 11.
But the master in order to be imitated must make himself agreeable to his pupils. " Vix autem dici potest, quanto libentius imitemur eos quibus favemus." "*It can hardly be expressed how much more willingly we imitate those persons whom we like:*" Idem, lib. ii. 2.

When we are not present with our pupils ourselves, we must entrust them—even in their play hours—to the oversight of those who will protect them from the inroads of evil.

All the rules which have now been stated, arise out of our first great principle, that we ought to carry on the work of education, as the vicegerents of that glorious Being who is Himself the Sovereign Trainer of his children; and that our work should be conducted in conformity to those gracious designs which he manifests by the order both of nature and providence.

It appears, therefore, that while these rules harmonize with the principles of Christianity, and are adapted to the duties of Christian educators, they are severally suggested by an enlightened view, even of natural religion; but it is to revealed religion alone, that we are indebted for the full manifestation of the doctrine that *God is love*, as well as of the practical consequences to which that doctrine leads. " God so loved the world that he gave his only-begotten Son"—here is the grand proof of the love of our Heavenly Father. But love begets love; and the Scriptures, while they unfold to us the scheme of redemption, plainly show us that love to him is at once our highest duty, and a motive of indispensable importance in all our actions. Again, they teach us, that under the influence of this motive, we are bound to observe the second great commandment, and to love our neighbour as ourselves.

These views suggest to us our next rule, the careful observance of which is well calculated to render the work of education effectual, because it has a constant tendency to make it delightful to each of the parties concerned in it.

X. Under the primary motive of love to God, we ought, in the whole work of education, to be actuated by love towards the objects of our care; and this love ought neither to be interrupted by passion, nor marred by selfishness. Aiming with undeviating steadiness at their true and permanent welfare, *love* will by no means exclude a hardy system of discipline; yet it will always seek their enjoyment in the *present*, so far as it consists with their greater happiness in the *future*. On the other hand, we ought to accustom our children or pupils to act on the same principles; without excluding the motives of hope and fear, (both of which have an important province in the divine economy,) we must lead them as far as possible to obey us, *because of their love*—first, to their

Maker and Redeemer, and secondly, to our selves.

Thus will our government over them be tender as well as strong; thus will their obedience to us be willing as well as exact. It will also be *uniform;* for while fear, for the most part, ceases to operate, when the party feared is absent, love "never faileth." The absence of those who are the objects of it, will sometimes be found even to enhance its efficacy.

The reader will have perceived from the whole tenor of the preceding remarks, that *education,* according to my view of it, is by no means the same thing as *instruction,* which it includes as one only of its essential parts. To teach our pupils science and literature, and to store their minds with useful knowledge, is indeed an object of great importance; but education embraces a far wider scope, and aims at the improvement of the whole man, body, intellect, and heart. On this ground, the following rule is worthy of our close attention.

XI. The care bestowed, in education, on these constituent parts of man's nature, ought to be applied *in its right proportions* — according to their respective practical importance, and according to that divinely appointed order, to which we have referred in a former rule. We must care for the bodies of our pupils so far as health, comfort, and propriety require. For their intellects our care must be more sedulous and emphatic, and it will certainly be one of our most interesting daily tasks to direct, illuminate, and enlarge all their rational faculties. But our chief endeavour must be to cherish in them those dispositions towards God and man, which lie at the root of a truly righteous and religious life, and which are necessary not only for a right performance of their temporal duties, but for their ETERNAL welfare and happiness. In order to this end, the Holy Scriptures are our most important and effective instrument. Our pupils ought to be carefully instructed in the contents of these divine records, and led to a daily use of them *in private*.

Our last rule applies to every branch of education, and crowns the whole subject.

XII. As our education of children ought to be in strict conformity to the will and purpose of our Father in heaven, manifested to us in Nature, in Providence, and in Scripture, so it should be conducted, in all its parts, and especially in the part last alluded to, in the feeling of unqualified dependence on *divine aid.* The educator ought, with all diligence of soul, to seek for the enlightening and enlivening influences of the Holy Spirit. These he will find to be the grand qualifying power, under which all his own faculties and acquirements will be rightly applied to the work which he has in hand. And having thus cast himself on the help of the LORD, he must quietly wait for the results of his efforts, even as " *the husbandman waiteth for the precious fruit of the earth, and hath long patience for it, until he receive the early and the latter rain.*"

SECTION II.

On Good Habits of Body.

The comfort of life, and even life itself, depend on some of those bodily actions which are the effect of habit, almost as certainly, though not so directly, as on involuntary organic motion itself. It is, therefore, a subject of gratitude to our Heavenly Father, that we learn to perform these actions, and to perform them *easily*, as a matter of course, and almost imperceptibly to ourselves. For the habit of masticating our food, for instance, and for the use of the limbs in handling, walking, and running, we are indebted to the force of nature, and next to nature, of example, much more than to the actual teaching of our fellow-men.

Nevertheless, there is business left for the parent or tutor in watching and directing the bodily habits of children. Bad habits, in the carriage of the person, in the management of the voice, in the turning of the eye, very easily insinuate themselves, and sometimes become fixed in the child, almost before they are noticed; yet they may often be prevented or counteracted by the early care of the watchful parent or nurse; and the confirmed lisper, stutterer, or squinter, has, in many cases, great reason to complain of those to whom was committed the training of his childhood.

It may not be wholly useless to offer a few remarks on the subject of *stooping*. The erect position of the body, and the manly fronting of the countenance, are among the most obvious marks which our Creator's hand has impressed upon us, of our superiority to the lower animals. They have an appropriate connexion with our appointed station, as intellectual and moral beings. Hence it follows that the formation, in young people, of an upright carriage, and of the habit of looking every man in the face, is a matter of no trifling importance. So far as it goes, it promotes mental vigour, a proper boldness of demeanour, and above all, openness and candour. Since no persons are so prone to stoop and hang down the head, as the indolent, the bashful, and the sly, stooping must be regarded as a sort of auxiliary to indolence, bashfulness, and slyness. For mental and moral reasons, therefore, as well as for assisting the easy play of the lungs, we must endeavour to guard our children against this awkward propensity.

The habit of an upright carriage of the head and shoulders, is useful in sitting as well as in standing or walking. Here it is opposed, not only to stooping, but to *lounging*. We might suppose that many robust young people in the present day, had been suddenly overtaken by the infirmities of extreme old age, were we to form a judgment, from their perpetual inclination to an indolent posture of their bodies—their neverfailing proneness to the use of sofas and easy chairs. Luxury, of a modern date, in the furniture of houses, has certainly thrown in their way many temptations to this mal-practice. But it will be found worth our while to cultivate in our families of children the opposite habit; for a young person who allows his body to lounge without restraint, will soon become a lounger in mind also. And when this effect is once produced, he will be unfitted for most of the purposes of business and duty.

There are few things in which the efficacy of habit is more perceptible than in *walking*. By habit this universal art is gained in infancy; by perpetual use, it is maintained in maturity. But some persons are *accustomed* to far greater exertions in walking than others; and distances which their neighbour would find it impossible to traverse in a single journey on foot, are by them surmounted with perfect ease. We must of course make due allowance for differences of bodily strength; but the superiority of power, in such cases, is mainly owing to habit. It would indeed be worse than folly to teach our young people to aim at the triumphs of the pedestrian; but many are the sons of study and business, who would be twice as vigorous as they now are in body, and possibly in mind also, had they been trained in the days of their youth to walk often, to walk far, and to walk well.

It is certainly desirable for young people of both sexes, that they should be early trained, when circumstances allow of it, in the practice of *riding on horseback;* and that they should be taught to ride securely and easily. In the first place, this practice is one of the principal conveniences of life; secondly, it greatly promotes the health, and assists the tone of the intellect and spirits, as well as the energy of the body; and thirdly, it seldom fails to give our children *pleasure*—an object, in itself, well worthy of attention. Yet this is a part of education, which requires considerable caution. The Christian parent who so much encourages the art of riding among his children, that his daughters become masculine, and his sons addicted to the hunt, will find, in the end, abundant cause to repent of his folly.

The manly exercise of the limbs in *swimming*, connected as it is with the immersion of the body in the water, is a healthy and invigorating practice; and when we consider how often it has been blessed by the Ruler of all things, as a means of rescuing his rational creatures from sudden death, we must confess that to teach our boys to swim, is nothing short of a duty. To neglect this object, is to refuse to avail ourselves of one of the links in the chain of a benevolent Providence. Let a man who is destitute of the power of swimming, be exposed to imminent danger at sea, within a short distance from land; or let him be standing on the shore, while some hapless fellow-creature, whom he *might* have delivered, is struggling with the waves, and he will find good reason to blame both himself and his parents, for the neglect of one of his talents.

We often hear that *dancing* produces a great effect in imparting vigour to the frame, and ease to its movements; but these objects may be accomplished by means of a variety of harmless exercises, and certainly they ought never to be pursued at the risk of moral injury. Religious parents who call to mind the temptations to vanity, as well as the trials of temper, with which the ball-room teems, and who reflect on the wantonness of giving up to dissipation those livelong hours which ought to be spent in *sleep* as a preparation for *duty*, will *shrink* from committing their boys and girls to the tutelage of a dancingmaster.

We have already found occasion to observe, that the *hand* is the appointed comrade of our intellectual powers. By the *hand* we avail ourselves of our reason, perform our purposes, and execute our arts; surely then a dexterous use of this organ may be reckoned among those bodily habits which adorn and facilitate life, and in which our young people ought to be carefully trained. Those who have suffered many an inconvenience from the want of *handiness*, may generally ascribe it to a defect in their education, full as much as to their native unskilfulness; and no persons will be more desirous that their children, after them, should labour under no such disadvantage.

Few circumstances make a greater difference

between one man and another, than the presence or absence of dexterity. For example, a surgeon may be deeply versed in anatomy; yet if he cannot make a ready use of his instruments, his practice will soon fall short of that of his *handy* brother, who boasts but little science.

But to look only at those demands upon our skill which naturally arise in the course of almost every man's life—what a convenience it is to be able to make an easy use of the hammer or chisel; to bridle, saddle, and harness our horses; to remedy any little injury which may occur to our carriage on a journey; to pack many articles in a small compass; to carve for a family neatly and quickly; to handle the oar or manage the sail when occasion may require it, and to *drive* with at least so much skill as may be the means of avoiding danger! Handiness is a qualification which runs through the whole of a man's circumstances; it renders his passage through this rough world considerably easier than it would otherwise be; above all, it helps him to maintain an honourable independence.

Nor ought the boy at school to be suffered to under-rate the importance of dexterity in *play*. It is greatly to the advantage of young people, with respect to the formation of their characters, that when they play they should do it well, and for a good purpose."* The tutor will be far indeed from losing his time, and may easily avoid the loss of his authority, while he mingles in the sports of his pupils, and sets them an example, both of activity and skill, in wielding the bat, or in throwing, bowling, or catching the ball.

This branch of our subject, however, appears to demand a passing remark of a moral and religious import. There is much of true philosophy, in the Scripture term, "clean hands." " Who shall ascend into the hill of the Lord, and who shall stand in his holy place? *He that hath clean hands* and a pure heart."† " *Cleanse your hands*, ye sinners, and purify your hearts, ye double-minded."‡ With an eminent degree of precision have the sacred writers kept in view,

---

* " Nec me offenderit lusus in pueris; est et hoc signum alacritatis; neque illum tristem semperque demissum sperare possum erectæ circa studia mentis fore, cum in hoc quoque maxime naturali ætatibus illis impetu jaceat. Modus tamen sit remissionibus, ne aut odium studiorum faciant negatæ, aut otii consuetudinem, nimiæ." " *Nor should I be offended by play, in boys, for it is a sign of alacrity. I cannot hope that the boy who is dull and hangs down his head, (in his play hours,) will be of an erect mind in his studies, since he falls flat in that kind of exertion which is so natural to his age. But let the hours of play be well measured, lest, if denied, they should produce a dislike of study, or if excessive, the habit of idleness:*" lib. i. 3.

† Psalm xxiv. 3, 4.   ‡ James iv. 8.

that as all evil thoughts and designs spring out of the heart, so it is the hand by which, very generally, they are carried into effect. A man of clean hands, is one who abstains from every deed polluted by fraud, malice, or impurity. When, therefore, we recommend to our young people the easy application of the hand to a vast variety of common purposes, we must never forget to enforce the necessity of *harmlessness* in all their pursuits; to warn them against that which is wrong, and that which leads to wrong; to teach them to listen to the voice of the inward monitor, when he is heard to say, " Thus far shalt thou go, but no farther."*

Cleanliness, in its literal sense, may certainly be numbered among good habits of body. It is needless to insist on its importance for the purposes of health, and for the personal comfort both of individuals and of families. But the mind has some part in this matter, both as to its origin and its effect. To make the most of that choice gift of nature, cold water, for the refreshment and cleansing of the person, requires some

---

* " Protinus ergo, ne quid cupide, ne quid improbe, ne quid impotenter faciat, monendus est puer." " *Therefore the boy is to be admonished, that he do nothing greedily, nothing wickedly, and nothing weakly :*" Quintil. Inst. Orat. lib. i. 3.

spirit and diligence; it is one of those lesser duties which the indolent part of mankind are prone to neglect. From all such laziness we must endeavour to preserve or reclaim our children; and we shall generally find that a daily effort to be clean will re-act upon their mental constitution, and, in some measure, promote the health of their souls, as well as bodies. Cleanliness of person ought, of course, to go hand in hand with a proper attention to decorum and neatness in attire. Such matters, when kept within their true bounds, are of greater consequence than many persons imagine. Young people who allow themselves the liberty of a slovenly appearance, will too often display analogous defects both in learning and conduct.

In connexion with the subject of *bodily habits*, it may be well to offer a remark or two on the due control of our appetites. That it is of the utmost importance for our welfare and happiness even in the present life, that these should be kept in right order, and indulged only on right occasions and in a right degree, is proved by multiplied experience. If reason and conscience do not rule the body—if their reign over it be partial and incomplete—much more if the true order of our faculties be reversed, and the body triumph over them both—bitter and evil wil. be the consequence. There will soon be an end of health and respectability; and, therefore, independently of higher matters, an end of all worldly comfort. Now the due regulation of the appetites must originate in the mind, and through the operation of the mind, (influenced of course by divine grace,) it must be carried on and perfected; nevertheless it is wonderfully aided by *good habits of body.*

Some persons are apt to say hard things of their bodies, and to lay their faults on their physical constitution; but *accustom* the body to sobriety and temperance, and it will presently cease to make the importunate demands upon us, which lead to the subversion of these qualities. The well ordered frame will no longer require any improper stimulants—the palate will lose its taste for the glowing liquor and the luscious dainty—the stomach will positively refuse an inordinate quantity either of food or beverage.

There is another propensity which requires a just and vigilant control, as well as appetites of a more active character—I mean the propensity to sleep. "Yet a little sleep, a little slumber—a little folding of the hands to sleep—so shall thy poverty come as one that travelleth, and thy want as an armed man."* *Early rising*, so far as health and strength allow of it, is unquestionably a bodily habit of great value, and bodily though it be, it is usually the result of a well ordered and energetic mind. At the rate of a single hour *per diem*, redeemed from the needless slumbers of the morning, the early riser adds fifteen days, consisting entirely of working hours, to every passing year—a number equal, for all active purposes, to a month of common days. What important economy is here—what an enlargement of opportunity for improving ourselves, for benefiting our fellow-men, and for serving our Creator! What a means of health and usefulness both for body and mind! Yet this desirable practice must not be overstrained. Sound sleep is a blessing which rests, with peculiar force and sweetness, on the eyelids of the young and uncontaminated. The great point in all such matters, is to observe the right medium. The play of nature ought to be at once vigorous and easy; nor will the *young Christian* give way to sloth, while he bears in mind the apostolic precept, "Whatsoever ye do, do it *heartily*, as unto the Lord, and not unto man."

* Prov. vi. 10, 11.

SECTION III.*

On Good Habits of Art.

In the course of the preceding remarks, the subject of *good habits of art* has been, in some degree, anticipated; for it is obvious that walking, riding, swimming, and the numberless common practices which call into action the quality of *handiness*, are all of them arts. Although executed by the body, they require corresponding exertions of the mind, and they are exercised under the sovereign orders of the will. Now, in all these matters, it is practice, and practice only, which makes perfect; difficulties fade away by the law of "passive impressions;" facilities increase, by that of "active habits."

But we must pursue the subject a little farther, in reference to certain arts which are commonly taught in families and schools. In some of these, genius occupies an important place; but habit asserts her sway over them *all*.

It is not my purpose to dwell on arts which belong to particular trades and professions; such as the various kinds of mechanism, surgery, agriculture, &c. These may be dismissed with the general remark, that the proper stage of youth for instruction in such pursuits, is neither infancy, nor early boyhood; but the last few years before the arrival of manhood. Our *children* must be trained in good principles and fundamental good habits; and on the nearer approach to maturity, when they are old enough to evince a decided tendency towards some particular avocation, we must place them under fresh training, in order to qualify them for their *specific* duties. Boys who are contemporary at school, are for the most part subject to the same system of education; but how many are the lines, according to the good order of Providence, in which they afterwards diverge! If the root of the tree be well watered, and the trunk be healthy, the branches, at the point of division, will shoot out with vigour in many different directions.

In considering the arts which are properly taught to *children*, we may commence with one which belongs chiefly to females. Time was, when in the education of girls, too many hours were bestowed on needle-work. To nimbleness of finger and correctness of embroidery, were sacrificed the cultivation of the understanding, and even the enlargement of the heart. But this does not appear to be the danger of the present day; and a caution is evidently required, that while our attention is mainly given to higher matters, our daughters should not be led to imagine that the needle may, without impropriety, be laid aside. To handle it well is both useful and *tasteful*—much more tasteful than to perform some higher art in a second-rate manner.* Those who call to mind the sober pleasures of the winter evening, when the females of a family are at work, while the father or brother reads aloud to the assembled circle, will be little disposed to under-rate the art of the sempstress.

There is no more curious proof of the effect of animal mechanics, and no more striking example of the power of habit, than is afforded by the art of *writing*. What a multitude of bones, joints,

---

* The idea of usefulness forms an important ingredient in questions of taste. A temple, in a pleasure ground, which is erected solely for ornament, and does not even profess to be of any use, is rather offensive than pleasing. But let the same building be applied to some useful or benevolent purpose—a school for example,—and we instantly allow that it is truly ornamental. Is not sewing for the poor, in our family parties, in better taste, as well as more desirable in other respects, than those lighter and far less useful descriptions of work, which are now so common?

muscles, and nerves are brought into harmonious and successful action, as each succeeding line lives under our pen! The perfection of handwriting consists, first, in clearness; secondly, in fluency; and thirdly, in *simple* beauty. A man, whose letters cannot be read with ease, is in the same class with his neighbour, who lisps or stammers in such a degree as to be scarcely intelligible. Since this is undeniably the fact, it is somewhat surprising that the art of *good writing* should be so little heeded in our classical schools—that it should seldom be practised in the higher classes of society—that it should in fact be considered vulgar, and fit only for clerks and men of business.* To the attainment of this art, however, a few lessons in Homer or Tacitus, in the course of the week, might be sacrificed with advantage; and since the time is evidently at hand, when the estimate of every branch of study will be formed upon its usefulness, it may

---

* The same neglect or prejudice appears to have prevailed among the Romans. "Non est aliena res," says Quintilian, "quae fere *ab honestis* negligi solet, cura bene et velociter scribendi; tardior stilus cogitationem moratur; rudis et confusus intellectu caret." "*Nor is the endeavour to write well and quickly (although generally neglected by gentlefolks) foreign to our purpose. A slow hand-writing delays the thoughts; an awkward and confused one, presents no meaning.*" Instit. Orat. lib. i. 1.

be presumed that such a sacrifice, when necessary, will ere long be cheerfully made.

With the art of writing well, must of course be united that of correct *orthography*—a point which ought to be well secured in the earlier stages of education. If neglected in youth, good spelling will mostly continue to be a desideratum, through every other period of life. Yet few things can be more awkward and inconvenient than such a result.

What art is so general, and yet so seldom performed as it ought to be, as that of *audible reading?* Let a passage full of excellence, either in prose or verse, be read aloud in succession, by several persons who have all enjoyed what is called a polite education. By most of them we shall hear it pronounced in a monotonous tone, with scarcely any regard to the pauses of the sentence, or to the modulation of the voice; and what is the consequence? An incapacity, on our parts, to attend to what is read—a tendency to wander away from the subject, or possibly to sleep, but none at all to listen. We might often be tempted to say to the reader, Understandest thou what thou readest? (ἆρά γε γινώσκεις ἃ ἀναγινώσκεις)* and

---

* Acts viii. 40.

we might in truth, suppose, that the subject of the passage had found no place in his mind and intellect. By some one of the party, on the contrary, we shall have the same sentences impressed on the ear, and through the ear on the mind, in all its excellence. Its meaning will become so clear as not to be mistaken, its beauty so perceptible as not to be disregarded. The cause of this change is the simple fact, that the present reader of the passage has thrown himself into the mind of its author, and by a due attention to pauses and modulation, has succeeded in presenting it to us, in its *native* force.

There is no book in the world, in the audible reading of which these differences become so striking or of so much consequence, as the Bible. The lofty strain of the prophet, the simple narrative of the evangelist, and the solemn doctrine of the apostle, may either lose much of their efficacy from a bad enunciation, or through a good one may be presented to the hearers with so much force and clearness, as to become doubly impressive. The voice and manner of the reader may supply the place of a comment. The daily reading of the Bible in families, is a practice of deep importance, and one which, I am happy to believe, is rapidly spreading. How desirable then that our young people should be accustomed to read it aloud with propriety, and feeling! I would not, however, be understood as pleading for any extravagant efforts to throw ourselves into the sentiments or scenes of the books which we read aloud. Such efforts are apt to produce a kind of acting, which is far from being either reasonable or agreeable. Audible reading, and especially that of the Bible, is never so pleasant as when it is natural, free from affectation on the one hand, and from undue familiarity on the other.*

---

* Quintilian warns us against a *hasty* method of reading. "Incredibile est quantum moræ lectioni, festinatione adjiciatur." "*It is incredible how much one is hindered in reading, by making too much haste:*" lib. i: 1. He truly observes that the art can only be taught in the act itself. "Superest lectio —in qua puer ut sciat ubi suspendere spiritum debeat, quo loco versum distinguere, ubi clauditur sensus, unde incipiet, quando attollenda vel submittenda sit vox, quid quoque flexu, quid lentius, celerius, lenius, dicendum, demonstrari nisi in opere ipso non potest. Unum est igitur quod in hac parte præcipiam, ut omnia ista facere possit, intelligat." "*In the art of reading, which remains to be considered, it can be shown to a child only in the act itself, where he is to pause; how he is to divide the sentence; where the sense stops, and where it begins; when the voice is to be raised, and when lowered; with what modulation each word is to be spoken, and what is to be pronounced slowly, quickly, or softly. The only direction which I have to give, on this subject, is that he should understand how he may be able to do all these things:*" Idem. i. 8. Certain it is, that *all these things* are essential to good reading.

During the many hours of the day which are devoted to the sedentary part of education, there ought to be seasons of comparative ease and relaxation. The bow must not be always fully bent, or the cord stretched to the extreme, and the boy and girl, even in the school-room, may justly claim their *horæ subsisivæ* hours, not of play indeed, but of diminished exertion. Several periods of this description may properly occur in the course of the week; and probably, they can scarcely be filled up better, than by the art of *drawing*. In boys this art is valuable, on account of the quietness and refinement to which it leads. In this way, it may afford a wholesome balance to tendencies of a rougher and lower nature, and will often be found an agreeable manual occupation in the evening family circle. We ought, however, to take care that drawing be made to serve some useful purpose; and such a purpose is answered, when it leads our young people to feel the pleasure of observing and contemplating nature. Sketching from nature produces, in this respect, a happy effect on the mind. How greatly may our sons or daughters enhance their pleasure in travelling through any beautiful country, by committing to their portfolios lasting mementos of its favourite scenery! Not only will such mementos be valuable at a future time, but the attention which they thus give to the objects delineated will heighten their sense of the various beauties with which a kind Providence has seen meet to adorn this lower world. It is a happy circumstance when young people are led by any innocent employment, " to look through nature, up to nature's God."

Here, perhaps, the reader will be ready to enquire whether I am prepared to make a similar allowance for a far more fascinating art—that of *music?* And if I do not reply in the affirmative, it is for this very reason—that it *is* far more fascinating. There is a great difference perceptible in children, respecting their taste or ear for music— a difference probably depending more on their bodily texture, than on the constitution of their minds. Now if girls have little or no " ear," it is an obvious folly to bring them under the discipline of the music master. Great is the toil which that discipline occasions, and almost innumerable the hours which it is apt to consume, and, after all, the effect produced is nothing better than those second-rate performances which can afford no pleasure to the true lovers of the art. In such instances, therefore, instruction in music appears to be forbidden, even by the laws of taste.

But let the state of the case be reversed—let our children have that delicate sensitiveness to sound, and that peculiar delight in vocal or instrumental harmony, which to many persons are evidently *natural*—shall we cultivate the talent, and give wings to the fascination? or shall we gently divert the taste and feelings of our pupils into some less exceptionable channel?

When I call to mind the corruption of the human heart, the follies and vices of the world, the enticements of the concert and the opera, and the easy access afforded, by superior skill in music, to the centre of fashionable life, I am constrained to confess that the latter appears to me to be much the safer alternative. I am acquainted with many families of young people, in which the study of music is entirely avoided; and I have sometimes been thrown in the way of other families, in which that study has been sedulously enforced and practised. I have observed that mental cultivation, practical usefulness, and sober domestic duties, are, in general, more prevalent in the former than in the latter class of families; and I can fully subscribe to a sentiment which was once expressed to me by the late excellent Hannah More, that it is no venial error on the part of serious professors of religion, to allow and encourage their daughters to spend those live-long hours, which might have been devoted to truly beneficial pursuits, in the ceaseless tiresome touch of the harpsichord or piano-forte.

Music, as commonly practised in the world, has often brightened the glare of fashion, seduced into folly and dissipation, fanned the spirit of party, and inflamed the violence of war. That it is far from being devoid of danger, therefore, in a moral and spiritual point of view, the reflecting Christian can scarcely deny; nor does it appear to promote the welfare of mankind even in the present life. Although productive of occasional pleasure, it seems, on the whole, to work in a direction opposed to our substantial happiness and comfort.

Before we quit the subject of habits of art, we may just glance at two of them, which are required to a much greater extent in the present day, than at any former period of man's history— *composition and public speaking.* Persons who have no intention to rank either as authors or as orators, are often obliged to express themselves in writing, beyond the limits of familiar correspondence; and in speech, beyond those of common conversation. Hence it is become more than ever necessary, that young people should be taught to compose not only grammatically, but with facility, force, and clearness; and our boys will be the better fitted for much of the business of life, if they are accustomed, *under judicious care*, to speak on practical subjects, in an easy and perspicuous manner. In both these respects, however, we must be careful to impress upon young people the value of modesty and simplicity. Neither reason nor religion gives any quarter to self-conceit; and the world is much too busy, patiently to bear with flourishes either in speech or writing.*

---

* " Nihil potest placere quod non decet." "*Nothing can please which does not suit the occasion:*" Quintil. lib. i. 11.

SECTION IV.

On Good Habits of Intellect.

Every one knows that to impart useful knowledge to our children, is a principal concern in the intellectual part of education; and no one who has been accustomed to the care of the young, can fail to be aware, that their capacities for receiving it are exceedingly various. The supply of information provided by the tutor, ought certainly to be sufficient to meet that fair demand for intellectual light, which arises from the general progress of knowledge in the world; nor ought it to fall very short of the mental capacity of the pupil; yet it is surely a prevalent error in the present day, to grasp at a great variety of knowledge in the education of our children—to diffuse our school-room teaching over a very wide and diversified surface.

Attempts of this description offend against the general principle, that education is in its nature prospective. Vain, for the most part, must be the teacher's effort to convert our children into men and women, and to impart to them that measure and scope of knowledge which belong to maturity; but when not vain, such an effort is far from being harmless. Just in proportion as we partially succeed in it, are we in danger of marring the mental constitution of the child, and of forcing a blossom which will soon prove itself barren. It is never to be forgotten, that our grand object in cultivating the intellects of children, is to fix in them those habits of investigation and study, which lie at the root of learning—habits of which they may *afterwards* avail themselves in ranging through many a field of literature and science.

On this ground I cannot entirely agree in the opinion of those persons who complain of the many hours, in each passing day, which are devoted, in most of our schools, to *Latin and Greek*. True indeed, it is, that a number of modern languages, and various branches of philosophy and science, appear at first sight to present superior claims, in point of utility; but I believe that no man who has imbibed, at school, an accurate knowledge of Latin and Greek, will regret the hours which have been devoted to the pursuit. Not only will he find the polish of classical literature a real advantage, and its treasures worth enjoying; not only will his acquaintance with these languages facilitate the acquirement of others; but the habits of study which he has obtained in the pursuit, will have given him a *mastery* over learning, which he will afterwards find it easy to apply to any of its departments.

There is, however, another principle against which this diffusive system offends; it is, that a little knowledge of an *exact and perfect character* is more valuable, for practical purposes, than much superficial learning. We mostly find that success in the world, and particularly in the walks of literature, depends upon a deep and accurate acquaintance with some particular object of pursuit or inquiry, far more than on extent and variety. By too widely spreading our efforts, we are very sure to hinder our progress.

It is essential that our children should be early instructed in the all-important lesson of learning what they *do* learn, *well*. If we sacrifice this object to a mere spread of information, we shall inflict an injury on their minds, which, in all probability, will be found incurable. A child who from day to day is allowed to be inaccurate and superficial in construing his Latin lesson, will be prone to act in the same manner with respect to the other branches of his learning, and his

15 *

carelessness will even extend to his play. But these are only the smaller parts of the mischief. The bad habit of *inaccuracy* once formed, will infect his mode of conversing, undermine his attention to truth, and weaken him in his moral duties; nay, it will follow him to the place of public worship, and mar the early fruits of his religion and piety.

The principle, that whatsoever children learn, they should learn *exactly*, is of equal importance whether their lessons be addressed to the memory, or to the understanding. If the business in hand is to get by rote a passage in the Latin grammar, or the declensions of a Greek verb, that business ought not to be passed over until it is perfectly accomplished. The memory must not be oppressed by too large a demand upon its powers; but the short and easy lesson must be so learned, as to be repeated without a fault and without difficulty. If, on the other hand, the tutor's object is to *explain* a rule in grammar, he must take care so to handle the subject, as to leave the understanding of his pupil in a condition of perfect clearness.

I am far from asserting that children ought never to get by rote what they do not at present fully understand. The memory may perhaps be sometimes profitably taxed, by way of adding to the materials which we shall afterwards bring to bear on the understanding; and in such a case a faultless repetition of the lesson will answer the general principle already laid down, that whatsoever the child learns, he is to learn *exactly;* but whensoever, in our teaching, we address ourselves to the intellect, we must take good care never to take a second step, until the first is effectually gained."*

I believe that this exact method of dealing with the understandings of children is very much practised in Scotland. "You Scotchmen," said a man of genius, to one of the professors of the University of Edinburgh, "are so fond of going round a thought, and round a thought, till you understand it all so precisely—for my part I love to see a subject illuminated *through a mist.*" The formation of such a taste as this person professed, ought to be carefully avoided in the education of children. To accustom them to the clearing away of the *mist* from every subject which they are required to understand, is absolutely essential

---

* "Nec ad ullius rei summam nisi præcedentibus initiis perveniri." " *There is no reaching the top of any thing without treading the first steps which lead to it:*" Quintil. de Instit. Orator. Proœm.

to their proficiency in learning, and even to their solidity in character. Such is the natural tendency of children to be superficial, that we need have no fears in adopting the Scottish method. By a variety of statements, all leading to the same point, and above all by apt and lively illustration, we must gently constrain them to "go round a thought, and round a thought," until it is entirely and accurately their own. Thus shall we possess ourselves of safe and solid ground, on which to place our forces for the next attempt.

The efforts of the tutor will however be all in vain, unless he obtain *attention* on the part of the pupil; and this is a point which will generally be found to depend on his own method of teaching. A man may teach in such a manner as almost to compel the most orderly child to be inattentive to his teaching; and his failure will only be made worse and worse, by his perpetual complaints against a fault which he has himself produced. The precept, the exclamation, the groan of impatience, will fall on the ear, and on the mind of the child, with less and less force, just in proportion as it is often repeated; and the result will be a total failure. But let the teacher secure, as his allies, the curiosity, the taste, and the natural ardour of children—let him play upon their minds, as a man plays on an instrument—let him make them feel the *pleasure* of conceiving a clear idea—and there will be few among them, so dull and careless as to refuse him an open an intelligent ear.

Whatsoever method, however, we find it best to pursue for the purpose, it is absolutely essential to our success in the education of children, that we should fix in their minds the *habit of attention*. The absent and wandering mind, the listening to what is read or spoken only in parts or patches; the indolent vacuity of thought when something is in hand to be learned, the division of the mind between two or more cotemporary objects of pursuit—must all be carefully discouraged, and if possible, *put to flight*.

When an eminent person, remarkable for his achievements in science, eloquence, and business, was asked by what means he was enabled to effect so much, he answered, " By being a *whole man* to one thing at a time." This is an expedient to which our young people ought to be familiarised even from their childhood. If their attention is scattered and divided, nothing will be learnt effectually, or executed well; but if they put forth their native energy to each object in succession—if they bestow their *whole* minds, first, (for example) on their Scripture reading, secondly, on their classical lesson, thirdly, on their arithmetic or geometry, and fourthly, on their game of trap-ball or cricket, every thing in its turn will be mastered; and by the whole process, the mind itself will be greatly strengthened.

A second rule which this person mentioned as having been of great use to himself, was never to lose *the passing opportunity*—a rule which, like the former, is closely connected with the faculty of attention. Our young people should be taught to be always alive to the circumstances which surround them; and in the only good and happy sense of the term, to be *timeservers*. It is desirable that they should be *observant* not only of their books, but of all things not sinful which meet their perception, in the passing scenery of life. By this means they will greatly increase their store of knowledge, and will be gradually prepared for usefulness in their day and generation.

The well known tale of the two lads who took the same walk in succession, the one seeing nothing, the other every thing, affords an apt illustration of the advantage of an observing eye, and of the blank occasioned by its absence. In an especial manner ought our children to be led, both by precept and example, to be attentive readers of the book of nature; to delight in her charms, to examine her wonders; to investigate, even for their amusement, her animal, vegetable, and mineral kingdoms, and to *trace the hand of God in every thing!*

There can be no doubt that there exist among children, as well as adults, constitutional differences, with respect to the powers of *memory.* The memory is affected by the condition of the brain; and the fact that one man can remember a whole discourse to which he has been listening, while another who has also heard it, can scarcely recall even its liveliest passages, may probably arise to a certain extent, from the difference of structure. But who does not know that the faculty of memory is capable of being cultivated, and that as a general rule, it is found to be true among children, that as is their *attention* to any thing, so is their *remembrance* of it. If a child has a lesson to get by heart, the facility with which he performs the task, mainly depends on the exclusion of roving thoughts, and on the resolute bending of his mind to the single object before him · and his power of afterwards recollecting what he has once committed to memory, may either be weakened by disuse, or strengthened by habitual exercise.

I once knew an aged prelate, remarkable for a lively and unclouded mind, whose stores of literature appeared to be always at his command. With the utmost facility, as occasion required it, yet without any appearance of pedantry, did he quote his favourite passages from Sophocles or Pindar, from Horace or Tacitus, from the best English poets, from Milton's prose works, or even from such authors as Erasmus and Grotius. It was easy and perhaps not unfair to ascribe to this individual, a structure of brain peculiarly fitted for memory; yet his friends were instructed by knowing that he owed the treasures of his age, mainly to the *habits* of his youth. When he was a boy at Winchester school, he undertook to commit to memory, within no very long period of time, twelve books of Homer's Iliad, six books of Virgil's Æneid, and several of Cicero's philosophical treatises. So completely did he succeed in the attempt, that at the expiration of the appointed time, no *dodging* could puzzle him. On the repetition of any one line or sentence in any of these writings, he could immediately repeat the next. Who can doubt that he triumphed over his prodigious task by the resolute and habitual application of his *undivided* powers?

A faithful remembrance and ready recollection of *things* are, of course, much more important than the memory of *words;* and are sometimes conspicuous in young people, who appear to have but little capacity for what is called *getting by heart.* Here, again, there is a close connexion between attention and remembrance. The more intensely we apply our minds to every particular which is added to our store of knowledge, the more it will be impressed upon our memory, and the more ready we shall be in recollecting it. In all such instances, however, the exercise of the memory very much depends on that of the understanding: the former will generally be retentive in proportion as the latter is clear. Present a certain fact or proposition—some new point of knowledge—to a pupil; engage his *whole* mind in the subject, though it be only for a short time; and take care that his understanding of it be full and precise; the idea will then assume a definite shape; and will seldom fail to deposit itself in the memory—ready to be recalled and fit for use, as occasion may require it.

In order to be a whole man to one thing at a

time, we must learn to exercise another useful habit—that of breaking our trains of thought, and of turning with ease from one subject of pursuit or study to another. This is a faculty for the use of which the rapid course of this busy world is apt to make a large demand upon us; and for the formation of which, in the young mind, that little world, a school, or even a system of private tuition, affords abundant opportunities. The minds of children are naturally versatile, and may, with little difficulty, be directed to various objects in succession. A spirited teacher, whose own mind is pliable enough for the purpose, may effect these transitions in the pursuits of his pupils with wonderful celerity—like the skilful mariner who shifts his sails, in tacking from point to point, with scarcely any impediment to the progress of the vessel. The variety of pursuit will, in fact, serve the purpose of recreation; especially if the harder and easier lessons are introduced alternately.*

Those who know the pain of being haunted by thoughts which belong to some past unpleasantness, and have no connexion with present

---

* "Adeo facilius est multa facere quam diu." "*So much easier is it to do many things, than to be long at work about one.*" Quintil. lib. i. 12.

duty, will feel the importance of accustoming their pupils to an *easy breaking of their trains*. They will be the first to appreciate that mental discipline, by which young persons may gain the happy art of turning their minds, without loss of time, from one object to another. One cannot but admire the prowess of a celebrated author, who, as it is said, wrote history one hour, belles lettres a second, and poetry a third; played with his children a fourth, and then wrote history again; and moreover performed all these functions with vigour and success.

Yet it must never be forgotten, that no men are so great in literature, in science, or in philanthrophy, as those who, while they give a fair attention to that vast diversity of objects, with which the world around them teems, have selected a leading one as peculiarly their own, and pursue it with undeviating determination, and ever recurring care and interest. A capacity for such selection, and such resolution, is indeed partly of a moral character; for it never fails to be connected with a *disposition* to decide and to persevere. But it is also partly intellectual, requiring first, a clear sight of the point before us; and secondly, that noble faculty of concentrating the mental powers, without which no man has ever occupied a truly elevated place in the rational world. This faculty of the intellect, as well as the moral qualities just now alluded to, have been remarkably displayed in their several and distinct pursuits, by a Galileo, a Newton, a Milton, a Porson, a Howard, and a Clarkson.

When the late Sir James Mackintosh was visiting the school for the deaf and dumb, at Paris, then under the care of the Abbé Sicard, he is said to have addressed this question, in writing, to one of the pupils — " Doth God reason?" The pupil for a short time appeared to be distressed and confused, but presently wrote on his slate the following answer; " To reason is to hesitate, to doubt, to inquire—it is the highest attribute of a *limited* intelligence. God sees all things, foresees all things, knows all things; therefore God doth not reason." True, indeed, it is, that the Omniscient Being who knows the beginning and the end, the cause and the consequence of all things, can scarcely be conceived to exercise a power of which the sole object is to investigate truth; but He has graciously bestowed this power upon man, and we are unquestionably accountable to Him for a diligent and fruitful use of it. How essential then, in the education of children, to cultivate their reasoning faculty, to teach them to mark its true limits and rightful application, and to imbue them with the *habit* of using it well! If we would impart stability to their knowledge, and raise them to their right place in the scale of intellectual beings, we must not only furnish them with information which they may take on trust, but accustom them, as far as may be, to find out truth for themselves.

By *reasoning*, however, I must not be understood as meaning the logic of the schools, which was productive of scarcely any other fruit than a useless war of words; I mean the application of our REASON to all the objects of perception and thought; and especially that mental process so perpetually required of every man, by which we *inquire into causes and consequences, and draw our conclusions, or form our judgment of things, from the premises before us.*

In this comprehensive sense of the term, reasoning is either inductive or deductive; it proceeds either upwards or downwards. *Inductive* reasoning commences with the observation of facts, and pursues its inquiries from effects to causes; its constant aim is to ascend from step to step, until it arrives at an original cause, or a general law.

Deductive reasoning begins either with a granted truth, or with a supposition, and descends from consequence to consequence, until it reaches that particular result which is the object of its search.

Both these kinds of reasoning are of great importance to the cause of science and truth, and find their way into numberless particulars in philosophy and learning. Take, as a familiar example, a boy at school, composing a sentence in his Latin exercises; he assumes the rules at the top of his page, deduces his consequences, applies these consequences to the series of words before him, and moulds the sentence into its proper shape. But let him parse what he has written, and he forthwith begins to reason in an opposite direction: the conditions of the several words are now to be regarded as effects, which he must trace to their causes, and by an inductive method he is soon brought back to their simplest forms, and to the rules from which he started.*

Mathematics, which afford the clearest examples of deductive reasoning, are, in their operation, at once perfect and limited. For example, in

---

* The pupil accepts the rules on the authority of his book of grammar, which for him is all-sufficient; but the grammarian who invented them, could have done so only by a like inductive method of reasoning, founded on a similar though more extensive observation of facts.

geometry, if the theorem be worked accurately, the result will be an infallible certainty; yet the truth at which we thus arrive, has nothing original or independent in its nature; it has respect only to the *supposition* on which the whole chain of reasoning depends. A similar remark applies to arithmetic, and to every other species of mathematical calculation. If our calculation be exact, and according to rule, our conclusion will be perfectly true; yet it can never be a general truth; it will in all cases be limited by the *datum*, with which our process commences.

To habituate young people to mathematical demonstration, and to the methods by which it is obtained, is obviously a desirable point in education. It can scarcely fail to invigorate their mental powers; to impress them with the beauty and excellence of an exact inquiry after truth; and to teach them a general lesson of precision, in drawing conclusions from premises; more especially, as their understandings ripen, they will find it a noble exercise of mind, to apply their mathematics to astronomy or optics, and to obtain a proof for themselves of the wondrous coincidence between the results of man's calculations, and the actual phenomena of visible nature.

Yet it is surely our duty to explain to our pupils, the limitations as well as the perfection of mathematical science, to show them its right province, and to make them thoroughly understand, that it is, from its very nature, utterly inapplicable to many important branches of the *inquiry after truth*. Who expects mathematical demonstration in chemistry or geology? And where would be the triumphs of astronomy itself, had not Newton arrived by observation and *inductive* reasoning, at a knowledge of those laws of gravitation, which are now taken for granted in every astronomical calculation?

Whewell, in his Bridgewater Treatise, has satisfactorily shewn that the great inductive philosophers, the original discoverers of the laws of nature, have been found universally believers in God; and no wonder; for in their researches into nature their faces are as it were turned towards the Creator, and they find it impossible to stop short of the first great cause. On the other hand, deductive philosophers, who are constantly engaged in arguing downwards from laws already discovered, have sometimes been found to forget that Almighty Being, who appears, in one sense, to be thrown into greater and greater distance, as they proceed in their inquiries. *Nature's law* is the beam upon which the whole chain of their reasoning is suspended, and by an habitual reliance on this alone, some of them have come at last to entertain the monstrous conception, that this beam is self-existent and supported by *nothing*.

One would think that this danger, in deductive philosophy, might be easily averted by the watchful and judicious teacher. In the meantime, it is obviously important that young people should be well imbued with the principles of *inductive* reasoning. Although we may have no wish to make them great philosophers, we should give them a clear view of those several steps which are essential to a successful inquiry into the secrets of nature. The first is to examine facts on a large scale, and with minute attention; the second is to analyse these facts with accuracy, and to reduce them to their simplest form; and the third, to draw *general conclusions* from them with caution and precision. This is the method by which every right minded inquirer into the laws of nature pursues his interesting course; and such an one will not fail to rise from cause to cause, until his understanding *rests* in God, as the Father of all things.

It is well that young people should be aware of the distinction between *formal* and *final* causes.

The formal cause of a thing is that by which the effect is produced; the final cause is its purpose, the object at which its author aims. Time was when philosophers paid such an exclusive attention to *final* causes, that the proper business of inductive science was impeded or prevented. That business is to trace the natural effect to the natural cause. The latter must then be regarded as an effect, the cause of which must be investigated in its turn; and this process may be safely continued, until we approach as near as our faculties will permit, to the simplest constituents and operations of nature. In the meantime, however, the observation of final causes—that is, of the fitting of means to ends—ought to occupy its own place in our minds, and to accompany us on our whole journey in the pursuit of physical truth. Thus while the inductive process is infallibly leading us upwards to the First Great Cause, we shall be instructed, as we proceed, by a countless multitude of *collateral* proofs of his existence, his wisdom, and his goodness.

But science is by no means the only field for the exercise of inductive reasoning; there is a *moral* as well as a physical world, to which it may be applied with excellent effect. What else is it, for example, which enables us to form a judgment, upon evidence, of the truth of any alleged fact?

To watch the proceedings which take place in courts of justice, may often afford our young people a valuable lesson. A man is tried for a felony: several of his neighbours come forward on the occasion, who witnessed a number of circumstances, with which the crime was connected. Their character is unexceptionable; and while the little varieties which appear in their statements plainly show that their testimony was not concerted, their general accordance, and the manner in which their stories *intersect* one another without contradiction, affords abundant evidence that they have told the truth. Their testimonies, considered separately, and the agreement of the whole, are so many facts or phenomena, before the court; and from these the judge justly infers the reality of the circumstances, to which they have deposed. He then analyses and compares these circumstances, considers their causes, and traces them upwards to that which can alone account for them —the guilt of the criminal. But now other witnesses come forward of equally good character, who were present when the crime was perpetrated. Their evidences, like those of the former witnesses, tally one with another in the most natural manner. From all quarters, direct and indirect, the rays of light are reflected on the crime of the prisoner, and there meet in a focus. The judge is perfectly satisfied, and directs the jury to find him *guilty*.

Who does not perceive that the conclusion, in such a case, although derived only from testimony and other moral evidence, is just as certain as the clear results of physical science? Nay, as a ground of action, it is evidently regarded as equivalent to mathematical proof; even life is sacrificed to it without hesitation!

Now let us suppose that the jury, in spite of this conclusive evidence and the consequent recommendation of the judge, should acquit the prisoner, and plead, as their excuse, that they cannot be *responsible for their belief*; would there not be a general burst of indignation? All the world would conclude either that they had neglected to listen to the evidence, or were prejudiced against the witnesses, or had harboured an immoral bias in favour of the prisoner or of his crime.

How vain then is the same excuse, when pleaded for want of faith in the truth of Christianity! Certainly we cannot furnish our young people with a more delightful exercise of their inductive reasoning, than in weighing the evidences by which its truth is proved.

Let them well understand the method by which the Christian advocate traces the evidence of written tradition backward from age to age, until he arrives at the *genuineness of the New Testament*. Let them next be led to examine the writers of that volume as so many witnesses; let them analyse and compare their testimony; let them observe the petty apparent differences which indicate the independence of these authors, and the substantial accordance, and more especially the curious fitting in of *oblique coincidences*, which prove their histories to be authentic; let them take into view the moral character of the evangelists and apostles; let them examine the collateral testimony of heathen writers; finally, let them dwell on those past and present facts —such, for example, as the early diffusion of Christianity, and the use among Christians of the first day of the week as their sabbath—for which it is impossible to account but by the truth of the Gospel history—and they will be *brought back* to the miracles and resurrection of Jesus, and be as sure of the reality of these events as if they had themselves beheld them. Nor can they stop here. From these signal interruptions in the order of nature, they will reason upwards to the power of Him who could alone have caused them. And what is the conclusion? That Christianity comes from God, and bears the unalterable stamp of His authority.

By another process of the same nature, and of equal extent, our young people may be taught to trace the genuineness of the prophecies, and to examine the historical facts, by which they have been fulfilled. From the wondrous agreement between the two, they will be constrained to infer, as a cause, the inspiration of the prophets; and from this they will again conclude that our religion is of divine origin. Now both these trains of reasoning are checked and confirmed by internal evidence. The religion which is thus attested by miracles and prophecy, is fitted with perfect exactness to the spiritual wants of mankind; it is on the side of integrity, purity, and peace; it abounds in the fruits of righteousness; its main characteristic is *love*. To whom then can they ascribe it, but to Him, whom nature and providence have already proclaimed to be not only almighty, but wise, holy, and beneficent? In cultivating the reasoning powers of our children, we must teach them, above every thing, to look towards God. They must be carefully instructed that true philosophy, both in physics and morals, will infallibly lead them upwards, step by step, to that "High and Holy one who inhabiteth eternity"—who fills, directs, and governs all things.

The habit of *reflection* is one, in which the reasoning powers are often called into useful exercise. To digest what we have seen or read, and thus to obtain distinct ideas; to recall and compare other ideas of a similar nature; to collect our thoughts into a focus; to infer causes or deduce consequences in the secret of our own minds; and finally to form a clear judgment on the matters which pass in succession before us— is the surest road to *intellectual wisdom*.

> "Knowledge and wisdom, far from being one,
> Have ofttimes no connexion. Knowledge dwells
> In heads replete with thoughts of other men;
> Wisdom in minds attentive to their own."
>
> *Cowper*

To meditate deeply and *think* with effect, is at once the most laborious,* and important part of study; and there can be no greater error committed in education, than to sacrifice the

---

* "Porro ut frequenter experti sumus, minus afflicit sensus fatigatio quam cogitatio." "*Moreover, as I have often found, thinking exhausts our feelings more than fagging.*" Quintilian, lib. i. 12.

opportunities of this exercise of mind, to a system of unnatural stimulants and rapid execution. Our children should be made to understand that to read without reflection—to fly over their pages—is one of the idlest of amusements; and that even a quick proficiency in learning is of far less value, than a stock of well digested ideas, and a sound and solid judgment.

In order to obtain these ends, young people will find it a useful practice to make notes of what they read, and even to commit to paper the *thoughts* which their reading suggests to them. This practice, which habit will soon render easy and pleasant, will check the roving indolence of their minds. It will oblige them to *think* properly, in order that they may *write* intelligibly.*

The habit of mind, which enables young people to embrace comprehensive views, and to form sound judgments, on the subjects of their study, will be required of them, for practical purposes, on manifold occasions of life. We ought to teach them that no two characters are more in contrast in the world, than that of a man who is prone to

---

* " In studiis præcipuum, quoque solo verus ille profectus et altis radicibus nixus paretur, scribere ipsum." " *Writing for oneself is a point, in study, of principal importance; the only means by which we can obtain a true and deeply-rooted proficiency in learning:*" Idem, lib. i. 1.

entertain hasty and partial notions of a subject, and that of another man, whose thoughts extend over a wide range, and who examines and delibe- rates before he decides. The great enemies of a sound judgment are *prejudice* and *passion;* and until we are rid of these foes, our intellect will never bear on the objects of our attention with its proper effect. How important then must it be, to train up our children in the habit of impartiality on the one hand, and of coolness and sobriety on the other! There is surely no capa- city of the human understanding so valuable for the purposes of the present life, as that of taking just and enlightened views of the circumstances in which we are placed, so that we may order our actions *wisely.*

The faculty of *wit* seems to lie in that mastery over the mental associations, which enables a man to seize on ideas widely different from each other, to bring them suddenly into contact, and to dis- play some extraordinary coincidence between them. Thus it appears, that the effect of true wit is to excite surprise as well as to produce laughter. This brilliant faculty, though somewhat rare, is *habitual* in some persons. The conversation of the late William Wilberforce was often enlivened

17*

by flashes of this description; but they were chaste as well as vivid, and wounded no man. It does not appear to be required of the Christian educator to *nip in the bud* that ready wit, for which even the young are sometimes remarkable; nor will he frown at those playful touches of *humour*—a faculty distinct from that of wit—which often diffuse a smile over the fireside circle. Yet these peculiar powers generally require to be checked, rather than fostered. No sooner do they run into excess than they become injurious. When wit is pointed into satire, and humour lowered into ridicule, they will no longer be tolerated by the teacher or the parent who aims at nothing so earnestly, in his pupils, as the improvement of the *heart*.

Nearly allied to wit is that fertile *fancy*, which enables some persons to adorn the subjects on which they write or speak, by images or illustrations drawn from natural objects or from common life. Such a fancy becomes active by habit, and will be found (as we have already hinted) a useful ally in the art of teaching; nor ought we to neglect the cultivation of it in young people themselves, because in after life it will afford them a certain sort of power over the minds of other men, which they may apply to beneficial purposes. It must, however, be remembered, that illustration is never to be employed instead of proof; that its sole purpose is to make an argument clear; and that for this purpose, it ought always to be borrowed from something more easy and familiar to the mind, than the subject which we wish to illustrate.

Imagination is a faculty which operates to a far wider extent than wit or fancy. It ranges over every thing which we have perceived and known, and which memory is able to recall, selects those particulars which please it best, and then by a magic art combines them into new forms; or to the true picture of some existing object, presented to the mind by *conception*, it will add some borrowed radiance, or some ideal horror, which imparts to it a character *above or beyond its own.*

We have already found occasion to observe the melancholy effects of the abuses of imagination. Yet there can be no question that it is bestowed upon mankind for wise and benevolent purposes. A child without imagination is a phlegmatic creature—difficult to be impressed; and it will be found a much easier task to educate his brother, in whom this faculty is somewhat excessive. A teacher may, in such a case, say with Quintilian, *Des quod amputem*—" *Give me something to cut off.*"*

Imagination may come to the aid of virtue as well as of vice. Dugald Stewart supposes two persons, in succession, to be introduced to some child of affliction and sorrow. They both see the same person and hear the same tale; but while the one draws no picture of his neighbour's unseen distress, the other, with his mind's eye, visits, in a moment, the wretched hovel, the bed of straw, the sick wife, the famished children. There can be no doubt which of the two will be likely to exercise the greater liberality.

The parable of the prodigal son, which has

---

* " Vitium utrumque; pejus tamen illud quod ex inopia, quam quod ex copia venit." " *Each of the two is a fault; but that which arises from want is worse than that which is produced by plenty.*" " Facile remedium est ubertatis; sterilia nullo labore vincuntur." "*The remedy for luxuriance is easy; but barren soils are overcome by no labour;*" lib. ii. 4. This author was well aware of the *detersive* qualities of true learning. " Nihilominus confitendum est etiam detrahere doctrinam aliquid, ut limam rudibus, et cotes hebetibus, et vino vetustatem; sed vitia detrahit; atque eo solo minus est quod literæ perpolierunt, quo melius." "*Nevertheless it must be confessed, that learning takes away something; as the file does from rough things, and the whetting-stone from blunt things, and age from wine: but it removes only faults: what literature has thoroughly polished, is less by that alone, through the loss of which it is better:* lib. ii. 12.

been productive of many a tear of penitence and love, is an appeal made by our Lord himself to the best feelings of the heart, through the medium of the imagination. And is it not the same faculty of which the sacred writers avail themselves, when they present to us a picture of all visible glorious things, in order to imbue us with some faint idea of the inconceivable glory of heaven?

Many of our Lord's discourses afford an evidence that it is neither unlawful nor undesirable, within certain limits, to make use of fiction in order to convey, in a pleasing and intelligible form, the lessons of truth. Yet it must be confessed that a method of instruction which by Him was adorned with delightful simplicity, and applied with unrivalled force, is in merely human hands prone to degenerate. Is there not reason to believe that the advantage derived from the moral of many a well intended tale, is overbalanced, in the minds of children, by the mischiefs of false colouring and undue excitement?

As our children advance in life, they may be tempted to indulge themselves in the perusal of novels, those lengthened and highly wrought fictions which fill our circulating libraries, and which for so many years past have been poured like a deluge on the British public. From such temptation we ought most carefully to guard them; for independently of the direct evil which many of these works contain, there is nothing more likely to unfit a young person for the duties and even the pleasures of common life, than the habit of living, by means of novel reading, in the highly painted scenes of an ideal world.*

The best and most harmless method of cultivating the imagination in children, is to bring them to an acquaintance with the most eminent and unexceptionable poets, and to lead them to admire the beauties with which their works abound. For example, Milton, Young, Montgomery, and above all, Cowper, afford us a delightful scope; but while we avail ourselves of these various resources, we must not forget to show to our

---

* I am aware that some persons, even of a serious cast, would make an exception in favour of a large set of semi-historical novels, which have of late years much occupied the attention of the public. It is sometimes said, that these works may serve the purpose of undermining the public taste for the more wretched and sickly productions of the same class; yet what young person is likely to be the better for spending his precious time in the perusal of a *multitude* of volumes which falsify history, and hold up a very imperfect standard both in religion and morals?

children, that there is no poetry in the world, so sublime and beautiful as the songs of inspiration, the poetry of Moses, David, and the Prophets.

In our attempts to cultivate the imagination of young people, we must carefully endeavour to chasten and refine it, and to give it a right direction. After all, however, the chief lesson which we shall find it necessary to teach them in reference to this subject, is to subject and regulate this subtle faculty, which, if let loose, will be sure to expose them to innumerable disadvantages.

Some of these are of a spiritual and moral nature. An imagination which spurns control, is the sure ally of superstition; it mars the simplicity of faith, it interferes with sobriety in conduct, it heightens the glare of vice, and gilds the baits of Satan. Others of its evil consequences relate, more particularly, to the understanding. By its delusive pictures and false colouring it seduces many a wanderer from the steady pursuit of knowledge; and it is the worst of enemies to that sober and intelligent apprehension of persons and things, which we usually denominate COMMON SENSE. On the contrary, this latter quality of the understanding deals with men and circumstances *as they are*. It neither exaggerates the evil which is in them, nor clothes them with a radiance foreign from their nature and character. It builds no "castles in the air," but is conversant with the common affairs and practices of life, and forms a reasonable estimate of their uses and consequences. It is neither despondent nor sanguine in its expectations of the future, but while it takes a calm view of that which is to come, it is chiefly engaged in a sober dealing with the realities of the present hour. This solid quality is of great value, in a world of change and perplexity, and like other faculties of the human mind, may become habitual through training and practice. Yet even a large endowment of *common sense* will be of little permanent avail, if we are not guided and governed by that divine influence, which can alone sanctify all our intellectual faculties, and elevate rational man to the station which he is intended to occupy both here and hereafter.

SECTION V.

On Good Moral Habits.

The moral nature of man has functions as distinct and clear as those of his intellect, and although the main object of these functions is to prepare him for eternity, and for that awful day when he must answer to the Judge of all the earth for the deeds done in the body, yet they are also intended to serve a most important purpose as it regards the present life. The right application of man's moral faculty is indeed of far greater importance to his happiness in the world, and to the welfare of those around him, than that of his intellectual powers; and, under divine grace, it is equally the result of mental discipline and *good habit*.

In treating of good moral habits, however, I shall begin with *mores* in the lowest sense of the word, and offer a few remarks on *good manners*. These are certainly of no small practical importance in the multiplied transactions and circumstances of this world, and ought to be carefully cultivated in young people; not only among the upper classes, but, so far as circumstances will allow, among those also, who belong to the middle and lower walks of life. Rough and untutored manners are injurious, as well as disagreeable, wherever they are found; and the tendency to them in man, who by nature is truly " like a wild ass's colt," may be easily counteracted in the supple days of youth, by judicious training.

No man, whatever may be his station in the world, has any right to annoy those around him by unpoliteness. It is due to society in all its relations, and in all its concentric circles, that we should be *civil* one to another. It is a great mistake to suppose that our least familiar friends and acquaintances, or those who are strangers to us, alone require at our hands the exercise of *courtesy*. This virtue, for virtue it is, must be carried into the nearest and most common domestic relations. Without formality, husbands ought to be *polite* to their wives, wives to their husbands, parents to their children, children to their parents, servants to their masters, masters to their servants. This oiling of the wheels of life, so easily obtained, so pleasant when in use, is grievously wanting in many a domestic circle, and the absence of it is almost sure to be productive, in the end, of serious breaches of family love and harmony.

In forming the manners of young people, we have, in the first and lowest place, to pay due attention to ease and propriety in the carriage and movements of the body. This is a subject to which we have already adverted. Closely connected with it, however, is a point at least partly mental — *shyness*, or its reverse — *a quiet self-possession*. It is very animating to see true modesty in young people, coupled, not with the bashful face hanging down upon the neck, but with the honest upright front which fears not to meet the eye of the person addressing or addressed. I have often been pleased with the union of these advantages, in the schools of the United States of North America, in which there is an air of independence to be observed among the children, blended with civility, which has given me both pleasure and satisfaction. We should never fail to impress upon the young a sense of the true dignity of human nature. Their courtesy one to another, and to their elders and superiors, will not be diminished by its being stamped on their feelings, by some master hand, that " an honest man's the noblest work of God ;" and that it is their duty and privilege to respect themselves, and not unduly to fear any man. At the same time these feelings ought ever to be tempered with that genuine diffidence, which ranges under the head of simplicity and humility—not of shyness.

Another point of primary importance in the formation of good manners is the cultivation of *tact.* A quick perception of that which is *suitable,* in our conversation and demeanour, to the circumstances in which we are placed, and to the persons by whom we are surrounded, is an invaluable faculty, and materially facilitates our course through the world. It is one means of producing pleasure and of avoiding pain, both for ourselves and others. The degree of this capacity in some persons, may be compared to the feeling of a hard skinned finger, and in others, to that of the tongue, which we all know is fraught with a most accurate sensitiveness to every thing which it touches. Yet this tongue-like sensitiveness has its dangers, and may lead, if we are not watchful, to a breach of good manners in another direction. It has need to be accompanied with the patience which bears and forbears, and with the charity which "is not easily provoked."

Here we are brought to a third point, which lies at the very foundation of good manners—the subjection of self, and hearty Christian kindness.

Benevolence is indeed the spring of true politeness; and the apostle has excellently coupled these things together, as belonging to one category. "Finally, be ye all of one mind, having compassion one of another; love as brethren, be pitiful, be *courteous.*"*

Next, in the order of our subject, to good manners, comes another quality, without which we can never take a smooth or agreeable course through this often troublesome world—I mean *good temper.* That temper partly depends on natural constitution cannot be questioned; for in schools and families we find among children, even among infants, a marked diversity in this respect, which must, in great measure, be traced to the peculiar frame both of mind and body. But although nature lies at the root of every variety of temper, much, very much may be effected by a judicious influence, training, and habit, in the cultivation of an easy and amiable temperament, and in the suppression of sullen, obstinate, or irritable humours.

These humours are like so many little demons, which haunt and beset the mind, and woe to that man over whom they so prevail, as to make

---

* 1 Peter iii. 8.

him their permanent habitation! Young people ought to be carefully taught, that every time the enemy is yielded to, he becomes stronger; and that whenever he is resisted, his power is abated. After repeated defeats, he will retire from the field, and leave the mind in that sound and peaceable condition, in which ability is experienced for every duty, and capacity for every rational and allowable pleasure. Let it ever be remembered, that ill tempers not only disturb the harmony of things below, but have a powerful tendency to prevent even an attempt to approach the throne of grace.

One remark remains to be offered on this subject. Although bad tempers partly arise from peculiar natural constitutions, yet, when yielded to, they presently lead to actual breaches of the divine law, and thus become absolutely sinful. Now for the sinfulness of man under any form, there is only one radical remedy—even the grace of our Lord Jesus Christ. Let it be remembered then, that *grace* is the proper cure for bad temper, and let this truth imbue all our educational efforts to subdue the evil in question. Let young persons be taught, when assailed by this temptation, to seek after retirement, and quietly to fix their souls on God their Father.

His Holy Spirit will then gently move upon their minds, smoothe down their asperities, and reduce the mountain waves to a calm level. The temper of Jesus was unruffled like that of the dove—blessed are they who follow in his footsteps. Yet this is no light or familiar business. A perfect cure of bad temper, as it is one of the most difficult, so it is often one of the *latest* triumphs of divine grace.

At the same time let no man mistake an amiable and kindly natural disposition for the saving work of grace. The good-natured and good-tempered among men require to be broken to pieces, and converted to God, like the rest of our species. Thus alone will the pride of their hearts be demolished, and their temper become not merely easy, but gracious—not merely smooth for the world, but suited to heaven.

If it is our duty to set a watch over our own temper, and to guard against all temptations to irritability in ourselves, it unquestionably becomes us to be careful not to vex or irritate others. Persons of very easy temper may often throw a stumbling block, in this respect, in the way of their friends, even of those with whom they are the most nearly connected. When for instance we fail in punctuality, and infringe on the time of other persons, by keeping them waiting in idle and unprofitable expectation, beyond an appointed hour — when perhaps, in addition, we are the means of spoiling their dinner and our own, and of destroying the wholesomeness of every one's food by half reducing it to a cinder—we really are guilty of more than one little crime. Not only do we break a contract expressed or understood, but careless and easy as we are ourselves, we excite an evil temper in those around us The man who has formed this habit of petty transgression will often find himself grievously belated, not only in the drawing rooms and at the dinner tables of his friends, but at the place of public worship; and *there* will become a disturber both of the serenity of his neighbours, and of a solemnity with which it is unjustifiable for any man to interfere.

Every thing is in some degree immoral, which unnecessarily interferes with the comfort of the social circle, of which we form a part. In this respect, the want of punctuality may be coupled with *absence of mind*. When some member of a fire-side circle is telling an anecdote, or reading aloud, an irrelevant question or remark, carelessly addressed *across him* by one of his hearers to another—the fruit of entire inattention to what he is uttering—is no small provocation; yet it is one which may often be observed. But absence of mind is one of those things which inflicts perpetual loss upon ourselves. We hear vocal discourses, or reading—the family reading of the Bible itself, for example—we may not be insensible to the interest of the occasion; nevertheless, our thoughts are roving the while through fields of imagination and fancy, and two-thirds or three-fourths of the words which fall upon our ears, so far as concerns our hearts and understandings, are scattered to the winds. We even frequent the Christian congregation, and profess to be engaged, with our neighbours, in the adoration of the Almighty; but our minds may nevertheless be floating hither and thither; and our worship, if such it may be called, is grievously weakened and marred. Thus it appears, that the precept already alluded to, that we should be *a whole man to one thing at a time*—or, in other words, that we should give our whole minds, in succession, to every duty and occasion as it passes—is not only necessary to the right exercise of intellect, but has an important part in the formation of sound *moral* habits.

There is no more irritating effect of *absence of mind*, than the inattention which we sometimes observe in children, to the commands of their parents or tutors; not so much indeed on grave subjects, as on a multitude of trivial and passing occasions. Twice or thrice perhaps have the words to be repeated, before the youngsters, engrossed by their own thoughts and eager pursuits, even hear them at all; and when they hear, they are little disposed to listen, much less to obey; whereas, if the order of families and schools is to be preserved, and a healthy moral tone to prevail in them, the hearing of the word of command must ever be ready, the listening exact, the obedience swift and unhesitating. The root of this evil is *rebellion ;* carelessness is only its surface, or cover, not its cause. Unquestionably it is at once the duty and privilege of parents to gain a complete victory over the wills of their children, in very early life — to decide the doubtful question, *who shall govern*, while that decision may be obtained at little cost—to habituate their offspring, from the first dawn of their intellects, to a ready subjection to all rightful human sway. Such an early habit of obedience will go far towards insuring the peace and comfort of the fire-side circle; it will render the subsequent work of the tutor or schoolmaster incomparably easier than is now generally the case; above all, it will be found the best preparation for that yoke of our Lord Jesus Christ, which is in truth PERFECT FREEDOM.

"Whatsoever thy hand findeth to do, do it with thy might," is a command given to us under the direct authority of the Holy Spirit, and certainly it is of vast importance both to our temporal and spiritual welfare. The applicability of this command to that large class of mankind who are compelled to earn their bread by the sweat of their brow, is obvious; but in order to form in these persons the *habit* of industry, in such a manner as to produce a good moral effect on the character, we must be careful that the stimulus which we apply be of a legitimate character—one consistent with the justice and benevolence of God. Nothing can be more demoralizing both to the master and the servant, than those stimulants to labour, which are the natural accompaniments of slavery—the severity of *ownership*, the whip of the driver, the terror of cruel punishment. Nothing can have been more happy in its moral effects upon both parties, than the change of such a system for freedom fairly tried, for justice and kindness in the master's rule, and for the due application of the motive of *wages*. When these are paid, not according to the time spent in work, but according to the quantity of work executed, it is surprising what vast feats of industry are accomplished, even by the much abused negro, and how completely the precept is fulfilled, to do what the hand findeth to do, " with *the might*."

Fair wages for work well performed is one of those provisions of natural justice, which has received the impressive sanction of the sacred writers — that is to say, of the unerring Spirit of the moral Governor of the universe. The infraction of this provision calls down in Scripture the severest reproof: " Behold, the hire of the labourers which have reaped down your fields, which is of you kept back by fraud, crieth: and the cries of them which have reaped are entered into the ears of the Lord of Sabaoth."* Such passages not only betray the radical iniquity of the whole system of slavery, but they apply, with a melancholy degree of force and accuracy, to that absence of due remuneration for useful labour, which is the stigma of our manufactures, and

---

* James v. 4.

often disgraces our agriculture also. We cannot indeed, say that the hire of these labourers is kept back by *fraud*, but we may truly assert, that a state of society, in which there is a vast accumulation of wealth and increase of luxury on the one hand, and most inadequate payment for labour on the other—with the grinding hand of poverty laid on the heads of untold multitudes —is fearfully at variance with the precepts of Scripture, and with all the wholesome tendencies of Christianity. Blessed indeed would that statesman be, who should discover a remedy for this tremendous evil, and apply it with a firm hand, in dependence on a God of justice and love!

But the industry of the mind is of greater importance than that which is chiefly or solely corporeal. It is made up of two qualities, *application and perseverance*, and it applies to every description of pursuit. Some persons find an extreme difficulty in applying their mental powers to any one pursuit in life with any degree of vigour; and when, weary and dissatisfied with themselves, they summon courage and make a rush on the paths of industry, they are soon appalled by the difficulties of the route, and fall back on that state of inaction and uselessness, which is, alas, their fixed and now insuperable habit. Such a state of things is generally the result of a careless and deficient education; yet it falls in with one of the most common propensities of our nature. A foreigner who had travelled extensively through many portions of the globe, was asked whether he observed that any one quality more than another, could be regarded as a common or universal characteristic of our species. He answered in broken English, "Me tink dat all men *love lazy!*"

C'est le premier pas qui coute. The chief reason why so little is accomplished, is that so little is attempted. To throw oneself into any undertaking, requires as much resolution as boarding a ship for an uncertain voyage. Things worthy of being done—things which we feel that we really *ought* to do—are constantly presenting themselves to the mind; but we secede from the trouble of determining to do them— we shrink from the *premier pas*. On all such occasions the spring of action truly required, and very generally missing, is faith in God. Children must be taught, in humble reliance on divine aid, to commit themselves to all the undertakings of duty, and boldly to attempt their best. The work begun, a steady continuance of mental application—an honest perseverance—

will seldom fail, under the divine blessing, to bring it to a happy conclusion; then the young person will be left at liberty, and in strength, for higher efforts and yet larger conquests over the *vis inertiæ*. Good habits in these respects have ever affected far more than brilliant talents; yet when good abilities and the force of industry are thoroughly united, who shall say what wonders may not be achieved?

While we endeavour to train up young people in the habit of industry, we must teach them to ascertain how much of exertion, whether of mind or body, each successive effort in the path of labour, study, or duty, truly requires. No more power than the object demands ought to be expended in the pursuit of it; otherwise the power is wasted, and the constant waste of power is sure to terminate, however gradually, in the entire loss of it. He who habitually gives his *pound* for that which might have been bought for his *penny*, will soon run through an ample fortune, and may probably find a home at last in the workhouse.

This remark may remind us of a virtue which ought ever to accompany industry as a twin sister—*economy*. This is a word of large meaning, and relates to other things besides money. Properly speaking, economy (οἰκονομία) is the regulation of the household, and he is a good economist, in a domestic point of view, who regulates his household aright—who has a place for every person, as well as for every thing under his hand, and takes good care that every such person or thing occupies that place; who admits of no waste, of no uselessness, of no disorder, in servant, child, or chattel; who adapts his mode of living not merely to his pecuniary means, but to all his circumstances and duties in life; and who maintains unbroken the harmony of the whole fabric (for every household is such) over which he presides.

As it relates to money, economy is by no means to be confounded with parsimony; it bears not merely on the saving of our gold and silver, but also on the right distribution of them. The well-known epitaph on a tomb at Doncaster is worthy the attention of every sound moralist—

> Wha! wha! who's here?
> I Robert of Doncaster—
> What I spent, that I had
> What I saved, that I lost,
> What I gave, that I HAVE.

Yet all that a man saves out of his income is by no means to be regarded as lost. Many persons, in various classes of life, are placed in such a situation, that the laying by of a certain proportion of their revenue, be the whole large or small, is an absolute duty; and indeed it would be a folly in any man, under any circumstances, to pitch his expenses at the full amount of his supposed income. We must all remember, that life is full of contingencies, and is by no means devoid of *exigencies*. Every one, therefore, from the peasant to the prince, should provide, if possible, a margin of safety; and there are many cases in which the proportion of income laid by ought to be considerable—especially when that income is the product of industry, skill, or trade, and not of property already in possession. The habit of saving a part of their incomes, however trifling the amount of them may be, is one in which young people, and even children, ought to be carefully trained. But to save *more* than our circumstances and duties require, is no economy; it is an act of avarice, and when confirmed by long habit, usually degenerates into the moral insanity and truly contemptible vice of the *miser*.

Economy dictates the laying by of such a proportion of our revenue as our circumstances justly demand; it also requires such a care and prudence —such true and well principled order—in our personal or family expenditure, as will leave a generous surplus to meet the calls of benevolence, in the promotion of both the temporal and spiritual needs of our fellow men. He is a good economist in a pecuniary point of view, who *saves* sufficiently, *spends* prudently, and *gives* with judgment, generosity, and effect. Extravagance or exaggeration in any one of these points, and in none of them more than in saving, is utterly at variance with the virtue for which we plead. It is, in fact, of the utmost importance to the moral welfare of our young people whose worldly circumstances are prosperous, that they should be led to form the habit of *giving* easily, liberally, and yet wisely.

The qualities of mind in reference to money, which Scripture chiefly condemns, are first the *love of it*, which is justly described as the root (or one root) of all evil, i. e. of all kinds of evil; and secondly *confidence* in it—" How hard is it for them who *trust* in riches to enter into the kingdom of God!"* These two qualities, which constitute that " covetousness which is idolatry," may sometimes be traced in persons whose sphere in life is very limited, as well as in their more

---

* 1 Tim. vi. 10, Mark x. 24.

opulent neighbours. It is also worthy of remark, that a man may be very little of a miser—nay, may be uncommonly profuse in his expenditure—and yet be deeply guilty of this idolatry—this worship of a false God—this service of mammon—this misplaced love and confidence. Again, the vice in question often betrays itself in dangerous and for the most part futile attempts to grow rich too quickly, and in trading for that purpose on too large a scale. Such bubbles are blown, and glitter only to burst; and often, as we may fear, the soul forms part of the possessions which we lose in consequence. In that case, who shall calculate the depth and horrors of our bankruptcy?

We have spoken of economy as the fit companion and comrade of industry. This is true of the economy of money. It is still more evidently so of the economy of time. The loss or waste of *time* is indeed a fault of perpetual recurrence, and greatly are *they* to be congratulated, who have learned the art of packing up life with precision and success. They still claim, and far more than others enjoy, their seasons of leisure; but every hour with them has its appropriate functions, and passing opportunities of obtaining or communicating good are seized as they occur, and turned to that profitable account for which Providence designs them. Such persons experience, in a happy and desirable sense, the truth of the proverb, "the hand of the diligent maketh rich." Not only are they enabled to make a reasonable provision for their own wants, but they are enriched above their neighbours in knowledge, virtue, and usefulness.

The economy of *thought* is another branch of the virtue in question, which is clearly connected with true industry. No tongue or pen is sufficient to set forth the awful extent in which *thought* is misapplied and wasted. Happy the young person who has learned the lesson of thinking well, and to good purpose! Happy he, whether young or old, from whose responsible soul, wicked thoughts in the first place, and vain thoughts in the next, are habitually excluded! But where are we to meet with this high attainment? Only in the watchful, humble, dependent Christian.

Prudence is assuredly a virtue of no mean importance, and the watchful application of it to the ever-varying affairs of life may certainly be accounted a good *moral* habit. As it relates to prudence, this world may almost be regarded, under the divine government, as one not merely of probation, but of swift and certain retribution. With respect to many glaring infractions of the law of God, we often see little, in the events of the present life, but a *tendency* to retribution— a tendency which is liable to be interrupted by natural circumstances and human power, and for the full completion of which we look forward, in faith, to the life to come. But the breach of *prudence*, though scarcely to be called a vice, is often visited with severe punishment *here*. Frequently is it followed by the loss of reputation, as well as of wealth and worldly comfort. The world is ever prone to take vengeance, even in persons of talent, benevolence, and piety, on the absence of discretion; nor will a generally prudent course be deemed to justify an occasional lapse. Many are they who can painfully understand the force of Solomon's wise saying, "Dead flies cause the ointment of the apothecary to send forth a stinking savour; so doth a little folly him that is in reputation for wisdom and honour."*

On the contrary, those who habitually "look before they leap," even in matters which appear to be of little comparative importance, will avoid

---

* Eccles. x. 1.

a multitude of disagreeables, and not a few distresses which would otherwise have fallen to their lot. Yet this habit of caution is carried to its right end only in those who add to it a power of acting, when they *do* act, with resolution and singleness of mind; to which may be added a dauntless perseverance. It is a weakening process to resolve and perform *hastily*, and afterwards to find ourselves compelled to measure back our own steps, or if this cannot be done, to cast " the longing, lingering look behind." Those who yield to these infirmities, though less criminal than Lot's wife, may find themselves turned into the pillar of salt—paralyzed for their onward journey, and for every wise and worthy purpose in life.

There is, as I believe, a divine visitation—a secret something, wiser and better than ourselves—which would keep us, if we would listen to its warnings, from things imprudent, as well as from things vicious. Socrates used to say, that whenever he felt inclined to mingle in the strife of politics, or to do any other foolish thing, he never failed to find himself checked by the φωνὴ δαίμονος, the voice of a superintending deity—a voice intelligibly heard *within*. Who shall say that this was not a warning from heaven? And who need doubt that those who humbly endeavour to become conformed to the divine will, will be enabled, if they wait for it, to hear the voice of the Spirit, respecting every proposed action of practical importance, saying to them, Do it, or Do it not? I may confess I have often felt the secret check, on such occasions, of *Do it not;* and when I have reasoned away the feeling, by proving to myself that the action in question was sinless, and so have done it, I have soon found, that sinless as it may have been, it was not *wise*. Probably many of my readers may plead guilty to the same charge of misdemeanor.

Solomon assures us that the " thoughts of every one that is *hasty* tend only to want."* He also declares that there is " more hope of a fool than of a man who is hasty in his *words*."† It is indeed surprising how much mischief a few words too quickly uttered—for instance, an expression of anger, the premature disclosure of an intention, or the blabbing of a secret—has often occasioned. That inward monitor of whom we have spoken, if duly attended to, would prevent those evils, by an habitual bridling of the tongue. " The tongue is a little member, but boasteth great things; behold how great a matter a little fire kindleth."‡

---

* Prov. xxi. 5.   † Prov. xxix. 20.   ‡ James iii. 5.

I remember that it was observed of a great and good man, who was zealous in his day for the cause of truth and righteousness, that he was not only wise in giving, but discreet in *keeping* counsel. Such discretion is a jewel of great value.

Here, however, we must not forget an important distinction. When prudence degenerates into *wariness*, and *wariness* becomes excessive, magnanimity and even honesty are often sacrificed to the habitual *noncommittal*. One cannot place the confidence justly due to a friend or a brother, in those who are always studying never to commit themselves. Such persons are thorough-paced self seekers, and their excess of wisdom may, in the end, turn out to be their poverty, and their folly. It is a blessed thing when young people are trained in the joint practice of caution and generosity, of prudence and courage. "God hath not given us the spirit of fear, but of power, and of love, and of a SOUND MIND."*

I was once acquainted with a person remarkable for sound sense, one of whose professed principles was to train up both his sons and daughters

---

* 2 Tim. i. 7.

in the habit of fearing nothing, so much as *fear;* and those who have suffered a multitude of inconveniences, and have undergone much pain in life, from undue fearfulness, will be the best able to appreciate the importance of such training. There can be no doubt that fear is very much connected with nervous sensibility, and this must vary according to the natural constitution. Where it is prominent in the character of a child—so that many little matters are fraught with terror, which have nothing in them to terrify—great care is required that our endeavours to remedy the evil be well directed and applied. The absence of severity, and of any thing in word or deed, which can shock the tender mind, must be carefully maintained; a steady, gentle, encouraging hand must at once support and guide the weakling, until the nerves become stronger, and the inner man braver. Every supposed danger quietly surmounted, will render the next wave that approaches less formidable, and thus a good measure of manliness and hardihood may be gradually acquired.

It is a sad habit of mind to destroy the happiness of the present, by anticipating future evil, and by imagining the approach of afflictions which are not, in truth, about to occur. Grace will be given to us, if we seek it, to support the trials of the passing day, or the passing hour; but if we take sorrow on ourselves by *forestalment*, we are not likely to be favoured with divine support under a burden of our own creation. Undue fear and anxiety are closely connected, and the habit of them both ought to be carefully shunned by all who wish well to their own happiness. Yet human nature is and will be weak, and I know of no adequate remedy for these evils, but the tender care of Him who is often pleased to interfere on behalf of his servants, and to say to the boisterous winds and waves, "Peace, be still."

We sometimes find in moments of exigency, when unexpectedly plunged into great danger, a feeling of quietness spread over the mind, which does not arise from our natural temperament, and which can be regarded only as the gift of a merciful Providence; but how few are able, at the very moment of surprisal, to take a clear view of the difficulties with which they are surrounded, to select the best means of remedy or escape, and to apply those means with vigour and effect! This presence of mind is an admirable quality, which cultivation may in some degree render habitual, and which, when become so, never fails to excite respect in those around us. No wonder indeed that all should esteem and applaud a quality which often enables individuals to protect and deliver their fellow men, as well as themselves, from impending ruin or death.

When at sea, I have been present on some occasions which have naturally suggested these remarks. Once, when our frail bark was struck with lightning, and was believed to be on fire, and when in the midst of a terrible thunder storm, there appeared to be but little hope of escape from the jaws of death, it was gratifying to observe the quietness which reigned among most of the passengers, including several females; it seemed to be a gift bestowed for the occasion. In the meantime our captain, though left nearly single-handed —for almost all the sailors deserted their duty and rushed into the cabin, displayed that undisturbed capacity both for judging and acting wisely to which, under Providence, we owed our preservation. There can be no doubt that, with him, this cool and effective management was the result not merely of mental constitution, but of repeated trial and habit.

Fortitude in bearing pain, either of mind or body, is a most reputable companion of courage; and where the sufferer not only endures the infliction with magnanimity, but wears the sunny smile during its continuance, divine grace may indeed be said to triumph over nature. Instances of this description are afforded, in abundance, by the history of Christian martyrs, whether they have suffered under the cruelty of heathen potentates, or of the fellow professors of their own faith. Probably none of these martyrs have displayed more of a holy fortitude than certain women. Mary Dyer, a member of the Society of Friends, who was hanged in New England for preaching the gospel to the people, nearly two hundred years ago, ascended the scaffold with a willing step, addressed her surrounding persecutors with calmness, and died in peace and joy. In sickness and sorrow, there are no braver sufferers than some of the softer sex; yet this bravery is usually connected with that gentle pliancy which dares not *defy* the storm, but yields to the pressure of affliction, and suffers the mighty wave to pass over and spend itself.

Sometimes, however, the wave is long in passing, or many waves speed their course in continued succession; and certainly there is no good quality more continually called into action—

and none, in which the force of habit operates more beneficially — than *patience*. I remember sitting beside the couch of a pious female, who, so far as she or her companions knew, *never slept.* She was liable to a perpetual succession of terrible convulsions, which, after the cessation of a minute or two between each paroxysm, would raise her violently from her bed, and when subsiding, would let her head fall as violently upon the pillow. This state of things had continued for many years, and I have lately heard that it is still continuing. But patience in the case of this afflicted one, confirmed, under divine grace, by long habit, appeared to be uninterrupted, and a bright ray of comfort on her countenance afforded a clear evidence that all was *peace within*.

Long continued sickness, with its usual accompaniments of bodily pain and infirmity of mind, does indeed often put patience to a close proof, both in the sufferers themselves, and in those whose duty it is to watch over them, and to minister to their wants. But let the guardians of the sick remember, that such afflictions are intended not only for the purification of those who are thus brought low, but for the instruction of all around them:

> "Smitten friends
> Are Angels sent on errands full of love;
> For us they languish, and for us they die:
> And shall they languish, shall they die in vain?"
> *Young.*

Persons who undertake extensive and distant missions in foreign lands will experience many a trial of the same virtue. Rough roads, slow travelling, calms at sea, and a multitude of other difficulties, including many an obstruction to the work in which they are engaged, will at once exercise, and if rightly borne, improve their patience. But as patience has its perfect work, they will find the truth of the inspired saying, "unto the upright, there ariseth light in the darkness. This quality, however, is sometimes almost equally necessary for those who seldom forsake their own homes; trials and provocations pursue us every where. Then let all who wish to live easily, and to pass their days in peace and quietness, seek after patience; for the best of men require to be furnished with it, whatsoever their calling, whatsoever their circumstances in life. "Ye have need of patience, that after ye have done the will of God, ye might receive the promise."* "Behold, we count them happy which endure: ye have heard of the patience of

---

* Heb. x. 36.

Job, and ye have seen the end of the Lord, that the Lord is very pitiful and of tender mercy."*

Probably there is no Christian virtue so nearly allied to patience as *humility*. The proud are ever apt to be impatient; they know not how to endure that their fellow men, or even divine Providence, should for a moment interrupt their serenity and happiness. On the other hand, it helps us vastly in bearing the contempt of our neighbours, and the infliction of all kinds of crosses by the holy hand of perfect wisdom and love, when we remember that not a trouble assails us, which we do not, in the sight of Heaven, most richly deserve—that we are poor, wretched, guilty earth-worms—mere pensioners of an hour on the bounty of our God, and depending for every blessing on his unmerited love—his gratuitous mercy. These truths cannot be too deeply impressed on the minds of children; the habit cannot be too carefully cherished in them, not indeed of the formal confession, but of the secret and abiding *feeling* of their own unworthiness. It works well with man in a moral point of view, and for the purposes of this life as well as for that which is to come, to be thoroughly

---

* James v. 11.

imbued with the doctrine of Jesus, "without *me* ye can do nothing." The foundation of true humility lies in the conviction of sin, and in a living sense of our need of a Saviour. This virtue, however, will never fail to lead us to prefer our fellow men in honour before ourselves. Such a preference of others is a sacrifice of the natural vanity and selfishness of the heart, to which young people ought to be accustomed; it is a habit of inestimable value. Yet a just self respect—the *par sui estimatio*—ought also to be instilled; then we shall have that union of diffidence with manliness, of unfeigned humility with an open, honest bearing, which never fails to conciliate respect, and which peculiarly fits a man to cope with circumstances of weight and importance.

In reviewing the points already mentioned, my young readers will, it is hoped, call to mind how needful for the comfort and happiness of mankind is the *habitual exercise* of courtesy, good temper, punctuality, ready attention and obedience to those who have the rule over us, industry, economy of money, of time, and of thought, prudence and discretion in word and deed, courage, fortitude, patience, and humility. I now propose to conclude this somewhat cursory essay, with a few remarks on temperance, truth, and benevolence.

1. Temperance. The "temperate" man of the New Testament (and this book contains the best of all codes of morals, both for life and for eternity) is ἐγκρατής, which means, "the man who has power *in* himself, *over* himself." Hence it follows, that the temperance (ἐγκράτεια) of Scripture is a most comprehensive virtue, embracing the whole scope of that internal government, which (under grace) it is our duty to exercise over our own propensities. Thus the fulfilment of this duty will entail, as a general result, a compliance with the apostle's precept—"Let your moderation (τὸ ἐπιεικὲς) be known unto all men, the Lord is at hand." For the τὸ ἐπιεικὲς, or *moderation*, in this passage, is equivalent to the τὸ πρέπον, *that which truly becometh*. It denotes not only a leniency towards our fellow men, but such a submission, on our own parts, to the dictates of infinite wisdom, as will lead to the keeping of all our propensities within their just limits—even in that blameless order which God has appointed. This is indeed a high attainment—one which the Greeks (and Paul after them) were accustomed to describe under the name of σωφροσύνη, which means not merely sobriety, but *sound mindedness*. To live under the regulation of this virtue (which comprehends

our whole duty to ourselves) is in apostolic language, as well as in that of the wiser heathen writers, to live σωφρόνως—*soberly;* i. e. in such a manner as a well regulated mind cannot fail to dictate.*

The practical operation of this most important quality is, in the first place, to restrain the whole man—body and soul—from things *unlawful.* There is a line of light drawn around us by the hand of God, which we cannot pass over without the commission of *sin,* and it is the first and most needful office of the virtue which we are now contemplating, so to regulate the natural propensities, as to keep them within this holy limit. In the exercise of this office, temperance may truly be said to make use of habit as her handmaid; for every single occasion on which the temptation is resisted, diminishes the power of the unruly passion, and adds strength to the virtue.

But scarcely less important is the next function of temperance—that of moderating the indulgence of natural desire or appetite in *things lawful,* an object for the securing of which good habit is equally essential. As it relates to the body, he only can be regarded as the temperate man, who

---

* Tit. ii. 12.

is accustomed and inured to this moderation; and possibly there are but few who are habituated to the true Christian standard, in this respect. Far be it from me to plead for the life of an ascetic, or for the churlish disuse of the bounties of Providence—much less for those self-inflicted crosses and mortifications which distinguish the children of superstition. But temperance, among Christian professors, in the point of view which I have now mentioned, has surely great need to be on the advance.

There is one example to which I am inclined to allude. It is an excellent thing, in my opinion, to accustom children and young people to total abstinence from fermented, and therefore intoxicating liquors. This abstinence becomes easy and even pleasant by habit, and it leaves both mind and body in a cool and favourable condition for all the functions and duties of life. It plucks up one of the most fruitful seeds of all manner of evil; or to change the metaphor, it lays the axe to one of the most vigorous roots of the "corrupt tree." Those who never use intoxicating drinks, are absolutely secure from the danger of abusing them; and when we consider how large, how varied, how insidious that danger is, it seems to be the part of wisdom to teach our young people wholly to avoid it. Nor is this obligation of propriety confined to the young. I well know that much allowance must be made for the long-formed habits of persons who are advanced in life; yet when we consider how vast a multitude of our fellow men are daily falling a sacrifice to intoxicating drink; when we behold the awful thronging of the workhouse, the madhouse, and the jail, which is the ascertained effect of such drink; when we carry our views farther, and think of the myriads, nay, millions, whom alcoholic beverages have been the means of plunging (as we have every reason to believe) into the bottomless depth of everlasting ruin—we are assuredly furnished with ample reasons for entirely disusing them. So far as our example can operate, let it operate on the safe side; and the astonishing fact that five millions of Irishmen, those native lovers of whiskey, have become total abstainers, affords abundant evidence that example does operate, in this matter, on a very large scale. Under these circumstances I am compelled to acknowledge—what until lately I was very unwilling to admit—that the apostle's principle of action fully applies to this great subject, "destroy not him with thy meat, for whom Christ died . . . . . for meat destroy not the work of God ...... it is good neither to eat flesh, NOR TO DRINK WINE, nor any thing whereby thy brother stumbleth, or is offended, (σκανδαλίζεται,) or is made weak."*

If a righteous control of the bodily appetites in eating and drinking, forms an important part of that habitual morality which is required of us as men, and as Christians, still more evidently necessary is such a control over other propensities of a more seductive nature. *Here* the line drawn around us, by the law of the Lord, is indeed clear and determinate; and the passing over of that line has produced, among mankind, a most awful amount of disease, misery, and crime. In numberless instances, as we have reason to believe, has it been the ruin both of body and soul. It is impossible too strongly to feel the necessity of training up our boys in habits of strict and unblemished virtue in this respect, and especially of inducing them, under a sense of the weakness and corruption of their fallen nature, not only to seek for strength to resist temptation, but for WISDOM TO AVOID IT. "Enter not into the path of the wicked, and go not in the way of evil men. AVOID IT,

---

* Rom. xiv. 15—21.

pass not by it, turn from it, and pass away."*

But temperance (ἐγκράτεια) applies to other things besides the functions and appetites of the body. This virtue lays, or ought to lay, her cooling, restraining hand, on pursuits and engagements of quite another character. A man may be intemperate in business, in literature, and even in philanthropy and religion. He may pass the boundaries of a righteous moderation in all these matters. He may become a slave to the desk, or a useless bookworm, or a spendthrift in charity, or a fanatic in things spiritual. There *is* such a thing as a "zeal not according to knowledge," which may be exercised under the plea of righteousness itself—a danger which Solomon probably had in view, when he warned his readers against being "righteous *overmuch:*" "Be not righteous overmuch . . . . . . for why shouldest thou destroy thyself?"† The righteousness which is "overmuch," is the righteousness (so called) which springs from the polluted fountain of the will and wisdom of man. But *true* righteousness is the blessed result of the influence of God's Holy Spirit. Of this divine influence we cannot have too much

---

* Prov. iv. 14, 15. † Eccles. vii. 16.

—we cannot avail ourselves of that which we have too largely. It is the water of life, let us drink of it abundantly. It is the breath of heaven, let us spread our sails to it without fear; let it carry our frail bark whithersoever it listeth; it will never harm us, it will never disorganize our mental harmonies, it will never destroy the right proportions in our feelings, our dispositions, our pursuits; it will never lead us to break—on the contrary, it will facilitate, establish, and confirm—the law of TEMPERANCE. In the truly temperate man—the happy child of ἐγκράτεια—the mind governs the body, grace regulates the mind, the creature obeys the voice of the Spirit, and the Creator reigns over all.

2. TRUTH. If any one point in moral culture, is important above all others, it is to impress on the minds of young persons an abiding and awful sense of the *sovereignty* of the law of truth. They ought to know and to be made to *feel* that this is a law which must rule and keep the mastery over all the dictates of selfishness or shame on the one hand and all the claims of politeness or kindness on the other. It is a law of which no expediency can justify the sacrifice; for "*all* liars shall have *their* part in the lake which burneth with fire and brimstone." The

devil was a liar from the beginning, and falsehood is peculiarly and pre-eminently his work and province. On the contrary, truth is one of the unchanging attributes of Deity; and Christ, who was the Word made flesh, is emphatically styled "The truth." There was "no unrighteousness," and therefore no want of veracity, in Him. A perfect integrity marked the whole of his conduct in word and deed—he was true, as God is true, and faithful, as God is faithful.

The *lie direct* is no uncommon fruit, in children, of the natural corruption of the human heart. Under the temptation of fear more especially, it is often uttered; and if not carefully checked and punished, it will become habitual, and will thus most dangerously infect the whole character. Those who are accustomed to visit prisons, and other abodes of criminals, must be well aware how entirely all regard to truth may be extinguished, and lying become a regular common-place practice, through the force of habit. More than a few instances have come under my notice, of criminals who have persevered in positive falsehood, (as there was every reason to consider it,) even to their latest breath. For such as these, how vain must have been a formal participation in the offices and ceremonies of religion!

The lie direct, however, is so universally discouraged by all reflecting parents, and so soon becomes disgraceful in the school, and even in the nursery, that it seldom continues to degrade young people of any class, who are tolerably educated; and among persons who are accustomed to cultivated society, it is too gross—too liable to be hooted out of the way—to have much place in the daily communications, even of the worldly and comparatively irreligious.

But lying in its more refined and seductive forms, is ever prone to insinuate itself into human conversation. Nothing is more easy and natural than to put a partially false colouring on any topic which may arise in our hourly intercourse with our fellow-men. We fear to offend them; we, therefore, tell them only half the truth, or the whole of it in such a garb as more than half conceals it from view, and thus we leave them, to some considerable extent, under a false impression. We desire to please them; we, therefore, give to our statements the peculiar *tint* (whether more or less precisely) to which their mental eye is accustomed. Or we think only of entertaining them, and, therefore, we exaggerate our pictures, and shoot (almost without knowing it) with the "long bow." There is also, many times, a want of perfect integrity in mere silence or concealment. We have, perhaps, something in our minds against a person, of which we may have little difficulty in speaking behind his back; but to himself we carefully avoid saying a syllable on the subject. In the mean time, if he is to judge by the ease and cordiality of our manners towards him, he must need suppose, that he stands perfectly well with us—nay, that he is without blemish in our sight. Now, it is certain, that such a course is directly contrary to the dictates both of sound charity, and true honesty.

These deviations from simple homely truth, are not to be classed with *white* lies, as they are called; there is no whiteness in them, for they involve a real wish and intention to deceive. As far as they go, therefore, they are black in their nature, and at variance with the eternal law of a righteous God. Yet they are of perpetual occurrence in the world; and there are few, perhaps, even of the more serious among mankind, who do not, at times, feel smitten by the rod of conscience for some measure of departure, in such matters, from the line of a perfect rectitude Highly important is it, therefore, for the virtue and welfare of our children, that we should train them, from the earliest dawn of their intellects, both in the love of truth, and in a deep, heartfelt sense of its *sovereignty*.

By " white lies," I suppose, may be meant those falsehoods which are so familiar, and so well understood, that they no longer *deceive*. But the term is one which truly belongs to the low standard of an evil world; for all falsehood, in whatsoever form it may be couched, whether more or less familiar, more or less efficacious in misleading others, is detestable in the sight of God. Deceit is its object and end, white though the world may call it. We cannot take a better example than the common worldly practice (less common, I trust, that in times past) of giving to the unwelcome guest, or the guest who arrives at an inconvenient moment, the answer, " Not at home," while the party visited is all the while snug and safe in his own study, or parlour, or chamber. Who can doubt that the moral standard of the domestics, in whose mouths this lie is almost daily placed by their masters, is miserably lowered by the commission which they bear? Who can doubt that such masters sin doubly before the Lord, first, in their own person, and secondly, in that of their servants — both in originating the lie, and in corrupting the agents of it?

The common parlance of the world, in many other matters of a still more familiar character, is notoriously false. Why should one gentleman style himself in his letters, the humble and obedient servant of another, when all the while, he would scorn to be subject to him even in the slightest particulars? Why should we apply to those around us a vast variety of titles and descriptions, which, however formal and *ex officio* they may now be considered, are, strictly speaking, "flattering titles," without any foundation, either in law or truth? Will not Christians cease from the use of such appellations, whenever the day shall arrive for the accomplishment of a very blessed prophecy—"Then will I turn to the people a pure language"—or, as in the margin, "a pure lip?"*

There is scarcely any purpose for which the love of truth, and genuine honesty of mind, are of more importance, than that of ascertaining *what the truth really is.* This can only be done by the impartial collecting or receiving of evidence, and by the just appreciation of that evidence when it is obtained. There can be no doubt, that the equitable care and strict impar-

---

* Zeph. iii. 9.

tiality which prevail, in this respect, in British courts of justice, are founded, to a great extent, on that well principled love of truth, and determination to maintain it in all matters of a forensic character, which has long marked the judges and jurors of this country. Yet our national annals are not without flagrant instances of the sacrifice of simple truth, to political bias, and even of the shedding, in consequence, of the blood of many innocent and honourable men.

The plain fact is, that a just use and appreciation of evidence, is ever found to depend on the state of the affections, and when these are warped by prejudice or passion, truth is no longer in dominion over us — she loses her rightful sovereignty; her influence becomes partial and defective, or is altogether paralyzed. When such is our condition of mind, the fabrics which we build in literature or science, in politics, or even in religion, are of little worth. They may, indeed, be ingeniously put together, and we may stoutly insist on their excellence and stability, as if truth, without any mixture of error, were entirely on our side. But in the day which shall make manifest every man's work " of what sort it is," the fire of the Lord will destroy them, as the " hay, wood, or stubble," and the TEMPLE of TRUTH—apart from all human prejudice, and constructed only of pure metal and precious stones—will arise in their room. This temple alone will be finally established by the hand of our God, and permanently filled with his glory.

3. BENEVOLENCE. This Christian virtue, so important for the purposes of life, and so essential in the character which can alone adapt us to the atmosphere of heaven, is founded, under the grace of God, on *sympathy*. It may be defined as good-will towards our fellow-creatures; it wills or desires their welfare and happiness, even as a man wills or desires the same benefits for himself. The benevolent man is he who habitually places himself in the position of others, so that he may feel their sorrows and joys, as if they were his own. Thus our Saviour commanded the true principle of benevolence to be carried into action, when he gave us his golden rule, " Whatsoever ye would that men should do to you, do ye even so to them."

If then we would educate our young people in the dispositions and practices of benevolence, we must study to form in their minds, in the days of their youthful tenderness, the habit of *sympathy*. It is true that the natural dispositions of children widely differ in this respect; but much may be done by the influence of parental care and instruction, and by consistent example. It is not very difficult to excite in them a feeling of sorrow for the afflictions of their fellow creatures—to teach them to place themselves in the room of the oppressed and unhappy, and thus to imbibe a sense of their woes. And yet there are principles in our corrupt nature in the fall, directly opposed to these feelings. A French philosopher has assured us—and with too much of truth— "*qu'il y a quelque chose qui vous ne déplait pas dans les malheurs de nos amis,*" that "there is something which does not displease us in the misfortunes of our friends." So far are we from naturally placing ourselves in their room, that we are prone to feel a secret satisfaction that they are depressed below ourselves in the scale of ease, honour, or happiness. Now this feeling is unquestionably wicked, and tends to the destruction of that good will to others, which is founded on sympathy. Let us pray to be delivered from all such sensations—momentary though they be—that our sympathies may be swift as lightning, and genial as the rays of an unclouded sun. Let us form the habit of placing ourselves mentally in the very condition of those whom we ought to pity—that our compassion may flow towards them freely and efficaciously.

Cruelty to dumb animals is exceedingly common in children; it is a part of that destructive nature which belongs to them in the fall. This cruelty cannot be too carefully counteracted. There is a just sympathy to be felt with the beasts of the earth, and with the fowls of the air. I am well aware that it is a law of divine benevolence as well as wisdom, that the lives of these creatures should be taken on many occasions—for the purpose of food, and for the prevention of injury. Nevertheless there are two principles in reference to this subject, which appertain, as I conceive, to Christian morality, and ought therefore to be carefully impressed on the minds of the young. The first is, that their lives should always be so taken as to put them to the least possible degree and duration of pain. Were this principle fully acted on, the knife or mallet of the butcher would be applied with a better-principled care than is now often the case; and the sufferings of animals preparatory to slaughter (for instance the hard and cruel driving of sheep and oxen, the repeated bleeding of calves, the conveyance of them in rough carts, with their heads hanging over its sides, and the odious cramming of Smithfield) would soon give way to a more enlightened and humane system. The gun of the shooter too — so prone to wound and maim — would presently be renounced; and in case of need might be replaced by the net of the fowler.

The other principle alluded to would, as I think, undermine the whole affair of *sporting* It is that we should never *make a pleasure* of the destruction of animal life. Were young people early imbued with this principle, they would soon find more innocent methods of healthy recreation than the chase and the *battu*, and I fully believe, that in the grand article of the formation of character, they would be great gainers by the change.

Sympathy, considered as the foundation of benevolence, is far indeed from being confined to " weeping with those who weep." The apostle also commands us to " rejoice with those who rejoice," and I am inclined to believe that this is the more difficult virtue of the two. Our French philosopher might have added to the remark already quoted, *qu'il y a quelque chose qui nous ne plait pas dans le bonheur de nos amis*, that " there is something which does not *please* us in the *happiness* of our friends." Our degenerate nature, full of pride and foolishness, shrinks from the notion that we fall below others, or that others are our rivals or superiors, even in prosperity and pleasure. But let it be our endeavour, both by precept and example, to habituate our children so to change places, as it were, with others, that they may forget themselves for the moment, and rejoice, with heartfelt feelings of satisfaction, in the joy of a brother, a neighbour, or a friend. Such is one of the most precious operations of true benevolence; it is a triumph over self, by which self is marvellously bettered. He who taught us to bless them which curse us, and to pray for them who persecute us, will enable us, if we endeavour to follow his footsteps, to exercise the sympathies of joy as well as of sorrow even towards our enemies.

It is not my purpose to travel over the almost boundless fields of the present subject. I wish only in conclusion to remind the reader, that the doctrine of passive impressions and of active principles, is in no department of morals more important than in relation to benevolence. *Benevolence* will decay if *beneficence* be not steadily maintained. Benevolence must be carried into act, daily and hourly, nay, almost momentarily, if we would preserve and improve this precious ingredient in the Christian character. Now action is far indeed from being confined to *deeds;* there is action for the mind in thought, and for the mind and body too, in words.

If benevolence then is to have due course in us, we must learn to *think kindly* of all men. We cannot indeed think *well* of all men; we must not confuse the eternal distinctions of right and wrong, or sacrifice truth to a mock charity; but think *kindly* of all men we may, and this ought to be our frame and our habit. Happy are they who, when they think of the fellows of their race, habitually discharge from their minds the stings of satire, and the venom of spleen! Happy they who, in the multitude of their thoughts within them, are more apt to dwell on the beam in their own eyes, than to perplex themselves with speculating on the mote in the eyes of a brother! Happy they who, while they dare not blind themselves to the faults of others, are ever ready to take a *fair* view of all that is excellent in those around them! In such persons benevolence is confirmed by a frequently recurring act of the mind; and while a virtue destined for heaven is thus strengthened and nourished, this present life brings far more of ease and pleasure in its train, than it can ever do for the satirical, the splenetic, the misanthropical.

To *backbite with the tongue* is a practice which Scripture visits with merited rebuke. It is opposed to justice as well as charity, for we have no more right to rob a man of his reputation and character, than we have to steal his property If our neighbour takes a wrong course, let us tell him of it face to face; very possibly he may satisfy us with his explanations—if not, we may perhaps restore an erring brother; but we must not make his faults the subject of our gossip with others; much less may we give currency, as thousands do, to evil reports of a friend or neighbour, which, when examined at their source, are found to be destitute of the slightest foundation. Let our young people be trained in the habit of avoiding this mischief, even in those lesser forms of oblique hints and significant inuendos, which a well-known writer on detraction describes as *pin-sticking*. Let us teach them, especially by example, to guard the character of their neighbours, and either to speak well of them, when the truth warrants it, or not to descant on their characters at all. It is a happy circumstance when our conversation has respect to things rather than persons, for here there is safety. In the meantime be it ever remembered, that charity in thought and word as well as deed is the "fulfilling of the law," and "the bond of perfectness."

But benevolence is more especially put forth into beneficence by *deeds*. We are in a miserable condition when the claims of our suffering fellow-mortals fail to have any influence in opening our purse-strings; and certainly it is cause for shame and humiliation, that multitudes of those who make a high profession of Christianity are as much afraid of untying those strings, for the benefit of their fellow-men, as if their very life was in their purses. This evil may be very much avoided by a careful training of young people in the habit, according to their means, of pecuniary liberality—a virtue which is then the most precious, when it is hidden from the view of our fellow-men—when even the right hand knoweth not what the left hand doeth. Yet we are not to forget that the giving of money forms but a small part of charity. There is the labour of love, the steadfast, persevering industry in the cause of the poor, the ignorant, and the unhappy, which far exceeds the careless pouring forth even of abundant alms. Nor ought this labour of love to be confined to objects of a temporal nature; it must extend itself to the loftier and more permanent interests of the soul. The philanthropist is often rather sneered at than applauded in this splenetic world; and some who have nobly devoted their best years to the benefit of their fellow-men, have become the favourite *butt* of worldly politicians and party newspapers. But such persecution is little worthy of regard. The unselfish, untiring, single-minded *Christian* philanthropist, is a noble type of our species; a blessing on earth, and blessed himself of heaven. For *him* benevolence is indeed carried into *effect*, and casts forth a new root into the earth, as every fresh effort is made to improve and benefit mankind.

Yet there is one truth of which the most active and devoted friends to mankind have need to be frequently reminded. It is a truth admirably couched in our Saviour's own words, "the poor ye have always with you, and whensoever ye will, ye may do them good, but ME ye have not always." Let those who are accustomed to all the acts of beneficence—those who give freely and labour diligently for the benefit of their fellow-men—those in whom the centrifugal force of charity has fairly balanced the centripetal tendencies even of legitimate self-love—never fail to remember that the Saviour who bought them with a price, has himself a paramount claim upon their talents, their time, and their affections. It is only as we are devoted in heart and soul to Him, depending on his grace, filled with his love, and formed on the model of his example—that we shall be enabled to *abound* in every good moral habit, so as to fulfil all the purposes of life, and finally be prepared for the enjoyments and services of a glorious and happy eternity.

There are, indeed, two observations of pre-eminent importance to the whole subject of *good moral habits*. While, in the first place, we are bound on every principle of sound policy as well as duty, diligently to cultivate these habits in ourselves and our children—while it would be at once injurious and sinful to fold our arms together in sleep, and supinely allow the enemy to sow those tares which will be sure to yield an abundant crop of vice and misery—this is a department in the field of human training, in which we ought peculiarly to feel, that in order to obtain success in our efforts, our dependence must be firmly fixed on the arm of divine wisdom, love, and power. If this dependence forms one of the most important principles of education in general, it is surely applicable with especial force to the formation of *virtuous character*. Here we have to feel and acknowledge all the strength and truth of our Saviour's saying, "Without me ye can do nothing."

In the second place, we ought always to keep in view, that true virtue or vice, in every man, depends on the state of the *heart*. "A good man out of the good treasure of his heart bringeth forth good things, and an evil man out of the evil treasure bringeth forth evil things."* What the evil treasure is of the human heart in the fall, we learn from another of our Lord's declarations—"Out of the heart proceed evil thoughts, murders, adulteries, fornications, thefts, false witness, blasphemies."† I have already endeavoured to show that the *bad* moral habits to which mankind are prone, and by which Satan so often succeeds in enslaving them unto death—palliated though they may be, and even arrested by human effort—can never be *eradicated* except by the searching, *penetrating* operation of the Spirit of truth and holiness; and that the religion of Jesus Christ, framed as it is with perfect wisdom, for the purpose of bringing our best motives into action, is the grand instrument in the divine hand, for reforming and renovating the moral character of mankind. Just on the same principles, it is undoubtedly true, that

---

* Matt. xii. 35. † Matt. xv. 19.

although *good* moral habits, in a worldly point of view, may to a great extent be implanted and nurtured by education, yet evangelical morality—even that holiness which can alone render us fit for enjoying the presence of the Lord, and for breathing heaven's pure element, is the effect of a *radical change of heart;* it is the triumph not of uninspired moral philosophy, even under its most excellent forms, but of simple, practical, VITAL Christianity.

SECTION VI.

On Good Religious Habits.

In attempting to take a view of good religious habits, as a distinct and supremely important branch of our subject, I am far indeed from intending to sever morality from religion, or religion from morality. I am fully aware that those good morals and good moral habits which are required of us as Christians—even those heavenly virtues without which we can never be fitted for an entrance into heaven itself—have their root in true religion; and further, that a profession of religion is utterly worthless in the sight of God and man, if it is not accompanied by that holiness, which is at once the genuine fruit and legitimate evidence of a heaven-born faith. Nevertheless there are certain good habits, of great importance to the formation of the Christian character, which are of a nature distinctly and emphatically *religious*, and there are certain habitual frames of mind also, which having a direct and peculiar relation to the Supreme Being, the only right object of religious worship, may be best treated of under the same head.

I cannot, however, with any propriety, enter on this department of our subject, without again adverting to the cardinal point alluded to at the close of the last section. If it is impossible for any man to habituate either himself or those under his care, to the exercise of true morality, without the aid of the Holy Spirit, so it is emphatically true of the *religious* man, that he is what he is " by the grace of God." The true Christian is the workmanship of the Lord Almighty; that new creation, to which he owes his spiritual existence, bespeaks the wisdom and power of Jehovah, just as clearly as the formation of his material organs, and the gift of his natural life; and his daily growth in grace is no more matter of human training and education, than is the gradual enlargement and strengthening of his bodily frame. Yet man may do something to promote the healthy action and improvement of the body; and no less certainly may he, when so enabled, co-operate with the saving work of grace in himself, and do much to cherish and promote it in others. In the formation of good religious habits we have our own part to perform, and have no excuse whatsoever for neglecting that part.

Rather must we exercise a holy diligence in order to this end, and then we may reverently expect that our Omnipotent Helper will bless our efforts, and bestow the increase.

1. It is an excellent custom—one which we cannot too steadily observe for ourselves, or too carefully promote in young persons under our care —*to retire into solitude*, from time to time, and especially at the commencement and conclusion of each passing day, for the purpose of close self-examination, and of communing, as ability may be afforded us, with our Father who is in heaven. "It is good for a man," as the prophet Jeremiah testifies, "that he bear the yoke in his youth. He sitteth *alone* and keepeth silence, because he hath borne it upon him; he putteth his mouth in the dust, if so be there may be hope."* That religious frame of mind, which is so beautifully depicted in this passage, can indeed be produced only by the humbling influences of the Holy Spirit; yet waiting upon the Lord in retirement is a *Christian habit,* which it is our bounden duty to cultivate. Our Saviour's precept on the subject of prayer is clear to the same point. " But thou, when thou prayest, *enter into thy*

---

* Lam. iii. 27—29.

closet, and when thou hast shut thy door, pray to thy Father which is in secret, and thy Father which seeth in secret, shall reward thee openly."* The Pharisees loved to pray "standing in the synagogues and in the corners of the streets," that they might be "seen of men;" but it is the privilege of the truly devotional Christian, frequently to retire into that privacy, in which he is under the notice of no human eye, and there to seek for ability to *present his fervent petitions unto Him,* from whose all-penetrating sight we can nowhere and never be concealed. Not only is the observance of such a practice required by the precept of Jesus, but it is in conformity with his recorded example. It was his custom, at seasons, and especially on the near approach of duties or exigencies of peculiar importance, to separate himself from his disciples, to retire into the solitary places of the garden, the wilderness, or the mountain, and privately to commune with his God and Father, in solemn, awful prayer.†

It is an animating truth that He who commanded and taught his disciples to pray, and who set them the example of private devotional exercise, is himself the all-availing Mediator, in

---

* Matt. vi. 6.
† Matt. xiv. 23. Luke vi. 12; xxii. 41.

whose name we are freely invited to present our petitions to the Father. "If ye shall ask any thing in my name, I will do it."* "Verily, verily, I say unto you, whatsoever ye shall ask the Father in my name, he will give it you. Hitherto ye have asked nothing in my name. Ask and ye shall receive, that your joy may be full."† In dependence on the advocacy of our adorable Redeemer, the Christian, when all around him is silence and solitude, will find it his dearest delight to commune with the Author of his being, and "in everything by prayer and supplication, with thanksgiving," to make his "requests known unto God."‡

Let no one imagine, however, that I am pleading for the offerings of the lip, which are not accompanied by the feelings of the heart; for those who draw near to God with their lips, while their hearts are far from him, are so far from bringing down his mercy upon their souls, that they are justly liable to his condemnation; like children who come to their parents with professions of regard and allegiance, which they do not feel, or, in other words, with a lie in their mouths. Such children must look, not for reward

---

* John xiv. 14.   † John xvi. 23, 24.   ‡ Phil. iv. 6.

but punishment; "the hope of the hypocrite shall perish." Prayer, in order to be well-pleasing to the Lord, and effectual for our benefit, must be heartfelt and sincere. When our hearts are truly touched with a sense of our poverty, our need, our helplessness, nay, our very wretchedness by nature, then, and then only, are we prepared to pour forth our petitions with holy fervour at the throne of grace; then, and then only, can we truly find access, through Christ, and by one Spirit, unto the Father. Certain it is, that we cannot pray aright without the " Spirit of grace and of supplications." " The Spirit also helpeth our infirmities, for we know not what we should pray for as we ought; but the Spirit itself maketh intercession for us with groanings which cannot be uttered; and he that searcheth the hearts knoweth what is the mind of the Spirit, because he maketh intercession for the saints according to the will of God."*

While the habit of frequent retirement from society for devotional purposes is one of a highly salutary character, we are not to forget that there is a solitude of soul, into which we may habitually retreat before the Lord, while we

---

* Rom. viii. 26, 27.

are engaged in the business of life, and are surrounded even by a multitude of our fellow-men. The watchful Christian, while he pursues his daily career through the world, never forgets that the Lord is nigh; he well knows where strength is to be found for every duty, and comfort in every care, perplexity, and sorrow; he is accustomed to introversion of mind, and is quick to feel the visitations of the spirit of prayer. These give rise to frequent living aspirations, which, though they be nothing more than the secret sigh, or the silent momentary ejaculation, ascend with acceptance into the ear of the Lord of Hosts, and bring down a blessing on the obedient follower of a crucified Saviour.

Finally, it is a blessed evidence of the work of grace in the soul, when Christians are found expressing prayer and praise by the whole tenor of their dispositions, their demeanour, and their conduct. Such an expression of *prayer* is found in that truly religious life which affords a palpable evidence that the individual is ever feeling, and thinking, and acting as a child in leading strings, fearing to take a single step alone, habitually depending, in all things, on an Omnipresent, Omnipotent, and most bountiful Father. And such an expression of *praise* is made manifest by the cheerful willing-hearted follower of the Lamb, whose every word and action bespeaks a spirit filled with gratitude to the Author of all his blessings. His heart glows and burns within him, and there can be no wonder that he runs well, for his race is the race of LOVE.

2. There are no persons to whom the habit of private devotion is more important than the heads of families, whose duty it is, like David, to walk before their house "with a perfect heart." If such persons are themselves acquainted with the benefit of communion with God, they will unquestionably feel that it is incumbent upon them to collect their children and servants together at least once in the day, that the whole family may unite in hearing a portion of Scripture, and in drawing near in spirit to that Almighty Being, whose "mercies are new every morning," whose "compassions fail not." This is a practice which has happily become very general among serious Christians of all denominations, and there can be little doubt that the blessing of the Lord rests on his servants and children who thus daily acknowledge him in their family circles. These have some satisfying experience of the truth of that ancient promise, "The Lord will create upon

every dwelling-place of Mount Zion, and upon her assemblies, a cloud and smoke by day, and the shining of a flaming fire by night; for upon all the glory shall be a defence. And there shall be a tabernacle for a shadow, in the day time, from the heat, and for a place of refuge, and for a covert from storm and from rain."*

3. Among those good religious habits in which it is our bounden duty to train up our families by example as well as precept, is the diligent attendance of congregational worship, whatsoever may be the section of the professing church of Christ, to which we are individually attached. This practice ought to be regarded, both by young and old, as a pleasure and a privilege, not a task. It is of the highest importance that our children should be imbued, from their very early years, with a relish for divine things—with a sense of their beauty and loveliness, as well as of their awful importance. A *devotional taste* may be formed in the young mind, through divine assistance, without much difficulty; and, when once formed, it will exclude the vitiated tastes of a world lying in wickedness. When a sense of

---

* Isaiah iv. 5, 6.

enjoyment comes to be associated with public worship, the habit of assembling with our brethren for the purpose, is formed of course; and as it becomes more and more confirmed, the relish of this reasonable service, if not heightened in its flavour, is at least strengthened in its efficacy. The more constantly we attend to so sacred a duty, the more necessary will it become to our *comfort*—the more substantial will be our *delight*, when we enter into the "gates" of the Lord "with thanksgiving, and into his courts with praise." Nor is it to be forgotten that the religion of the closet—the persevering devotion of the private hour—is an important preparation for that fervency and heavenly mindedness in congregational worship, without which it will effect but little for the permanent benefit of our souls.

I have reason to be thankful that I was trained from very early years in the *habit* of uniting with my friends in public worship, some one morning in the middle part of the week, as well as on the sabbath day. Thus to break away from the cares and pursuits of business, at a time when the world around us is full of them, I have found to be peculiarly salutary; and I believe I might assert with truth, that the many hours so spent have formed one of the happiest as well as most edifying portions of my life. Sure I am that such hours will not be lost time to any seriously disposed persons, but will lead to a better performance even of their temporal duties, than would otherwise have been the case. That the same remark applies, in full force, to the right observance of the sabbath itself, will be freely acknowledged by all who know and feel its value.

Far indeed am I from pleading for the actual sacredness of any one day of the week above another, or for that legal and ceremonial strictness with which this institution was observed, under the law of Moses. I fully allow that so far as that law was either civil or ceremonial, it is now abolished, and therefore not obligatory on Christians. Nevertheless, I am clearly of the judgment that the setting apart of every seventh day, for the blessed purposes of rest and worship, is a divine institution—one which originated in God's own Sabbath after the creation, when he blessed and hallowed the seventh day of rest after the six days of action—one which, in point of authority, pervades all time, and attaches to the whole family of man.

That no blessing rests on the desecration of this day all experience proves. Those who have seen it, under the curse of West Indian slavery, wrested from its legitimate purposes, and turned into a day of traffic and dissipation;—those who have watched the effect, among both Protestant and Roman Catholic nations on the continent of Europe, of the open shops on that day, even during the hours of worship, and of the formal religious service of the morning, followed up by the thronged theatre of the evening;—those who have known men of great intellect, who, in consequence (in part at least) of never allowing themselves the " seventh day's rest," have at last been so shattered in mind as to commit self-murder, (and all these circumstances have come under my own notice,)—will be little disposed to undervalue this divine ordinance, or to lower its position to the shelf of a *mere expediency.*

Let us then carefully cherish, both in ourselves and in those under our care, a reverent regard for the provision which the Creator has thus mercifully made for the relief and help both of our bodies and souls—for the winding up of a framework which may well be compared to the delicate machinery of a watch or clock; and let this weekly recurring day be *habitually* devoted to *waiting on the Lord.* " Although the youths may faint and be weary, and the young men utterly fail, yet they that wait on the Lord shall RENEW THEIR STRENGTH; they shall mount up with wings as eagles; they shall run and not be weary, and they shall walk and not faint."*

4. The Bible is not given to us as a sealed book which we have no right to open when we please, or to study without the intervention of some ecclesiastical guide. It is a treasure which was never placed by Divine Providence under the key of a priesthood, but is one of the free gifts of God to man, graciously adapted by the Author of our being, to the whole of our fallen race. It is indeed an admirable evidence of the truth and divine origin of the Sacred Volume, that for its most important practical purposes—especially for the great end of the soul's salvation—it is just as intelligible to the humble but pious cottager, as it is to the most learned and cultivated among mankind. The rough Greenlander and Esquimaux, the untutored inhabitant of New Zealand or Otaheite, the wandering North American Indian, the superstitious and degraded Hindoo and Chinese, the Hottentot of South Africa, the Negro and Malagassee—ignorant and uncultivated

---

* Isaiah xl 31.

men in almost every part of the world—have all been found capable, with the aid of the most simple Christian teaching, of understanding the Holy Scriptures, so far as relates to their main purpose—I mean that of instructing us in the knowledge of God and of Jesus Christ our Lord; and the same book has been the means of imparting the same knowledge to the polite and civilized Greek and Roman, as well as to the Bacons, Lockes, Boyles, Addisons, and Newtons of modern times—the most refined and philosophcial of our species.

Among good religious habits, the frequent and careful perusal of this best of all books assumes a highly important place. Our young people cannot be habituated to a more profitable line of acquaintance, than that which leads to an intimacy of soul with prophets, evangelists, and apostles, and above all, with the Lord Jesus, whose example, character, and doctrine, are brought before us, in the most vivid manner, in the four gospels. The daily *private* reading of Scripture ought, therefore, to be a primary object in Christian education. In following this pursuit, we shall find it a great advantage to peruse the Sacred Volume in its original languages. The Hebrew of the Old Testament is accessible, without difficulty, to every persevering student, and the Greek, which is so commonly taught in our schools, cannot be better applied, as we advance in life, than in the use of that precious volume, the Greek Testament. Independently of the consideration of its divine origin, the writings which it contains are of unrivalled force, beauty and simplicity. Yet, doubtless, it *is* its divine origin which imparts to it the sweetness of its savour, and the strength of its charm. Here are the morals and here the doctrines of heaven; here is a history most graphical in its touches, and most teaching in its tendency; here are prophecies which develop that mighty struggle between good and evil, between light and darkness, which has been going on, in this world of alternations, during the last eighteen centuries, and which is destined to result in the final triumph of truth and holiness. Here, above all, is presented to us the Lord Jesus Christ, the man of sorrows, the herald of peace, the pattern of virtue, the one great sacrifice for sin suffering and triumphant, dying and living again, and now for ever exalted at the right hand of the Father, to be our Advocate with Him.

Let not those, however, who cannot enjoy the privilege of reading the Scriptures in their original form, imagine for a moment that they are *at fault* with only the common English version in their hands. It is an admirable translation, dignified, clear, forcible, and generally accurate. Well may we be thankful to that Divine Providence which has led to its being so far established, by custom rather than authority, as to have become, in effect, the one version used by all who speak the language of this country. Such a provision is far more favourable to the cause of religion, than the distraction which would be occasioned by the competition of many translations of the Bible into our language, however excellent any of them might be.

The young and well-trained member of a household, who is accustomed to the private perusal of Scripture on rising in the morning, and before he retires to rest at night, and who hears it read, or reads it himself, daily in the family circle, is in the way of obtaining an *accurate* knowledge of its contents — a knowledge which he has been led to acquire by a love of the truth, and by which that love cannot fail to be confirmed. Here, however, I would advise my young friends, of every name and class, never to pass a day without committing a small portion of the Sacred Volume to memory. The records of the Bible Society contain accounts of great attainments in this line of divine learning. It has sometimes happened, that young Roman Catholics in Ireland have got by heart whole books of the New Testament, and thus, when afterwards deprived by their ecclesiastical guides of the Sacred Volume, they have found themselves in happy possession of a large part of its contents. The Abyssinian Scriptures are said to have been used in the same manner, and with the same success; and certainly it ought to be a very general practice. Those who thus learn the Scriptures, make them their *own* in a double degree; and passages, well committed to memory in early life, will generally remain in it, even to old age. Early life is the period for such exercises of a faculty, which is almost sure to lose its power of retention as business multiplies, and *the brain grows old*.

5. There are two points which ought to be habitually observed in the reading and interpretation of the Sacred Volume. The first is that *broad impartiality* which prefers simple truth to any preconceived opinions, and to any human system. The second is a reverent dependence on the illuminating influence of the Holy Spirit. "I have long pursued the study of Scripture,"

said an aged and revered friend of mine long since deceased, "with a desire to be impartial. I commit myself to the teaching of the inspired writers, whatsoever complexion it may assume. One thing I know assuredly, that in religion, of myself, I *know nothing*. I do not, therefore, sit down to the perusal of Scripture, in order to *impose* a sense on the prophets and apostles, but to *receive* one as they give it me. I pretend not to teach them; I wish like a child to be taught *by* them."

This principle of childlike submission to divine authority, and of an even-handed equity in the reception and appreciation of the contents of Holy Scripture, has no more important application than to those cardinal subjects, *justification and sanctification*. It has always appeared to me that the glad tidings of salvation, which are declared to us in Scripture, and especially in the New Testament, principally consist of two leading and essential parts, equal to each other in magnitude and importance, and although distinct in their nature and character, yet perfectly accordant, and combined by an inseparable union in God's own mighty plan for the redemption of mankind.

The first of these parts finds its centre in the doctrine of the Atonement, and relates to that which our Lord Jesus Christ has already done for us of his own voluntary love and mercy, and wholly independently of ourselves. He hath "trodden the winepress ALONE, and of the people there was none" with him. "He is the propitiation (or expiatory sacrifice) for our sins;" and through this all-availing offering of Jesus on the cross, we who are "by nature the children of wrath," receive the forgiveness of our sins, and are reconciled to a just and holy God. The second grand constituent of the gospel of Christ, is the promise of the Holy Spirit, and the whole doctrine of his enlightening, enlivening, and sanctifying influences. It is by these influences that the living and reigning Saviour visits our dark hearts, convinces of sin, bestows the grace of repentance, converts to a living faith in himself, and carries on that necessary work of inward purification, which can alone prepare us for a state of eternal holiness, peace, and joy.

If, in the perusal of Holy Writ, we dwell on the former of these subjects to the exclusion of the latter, we shall soon fall into antinomianism; and if on the latter to the exclusion of the former, we shall be in danger of being weighed down, even unto destruction, by the burden of our past sins. We stand in absolute need of the pardon of our past transgressions through the atoning sacrifice of Jesus; and equally do we require a deliverance from present sin, by the power of the Holy Spirit. Let us then cleave, with equal love, and zeal, and reverence, to both these branches of divine truth. Justification and sanctification are joined together by the hand of our God, and must never be dissevered. If one of them occupy a less space in our minds and feelings than the other, our Christianity will soon become defective or distorted, just in the degree in which the holy balance between them is sacrificed and lost. Can anything be more clear or more emphatic than the numerous passages of Scripture, in which the sacred writers, and our Saviour himself in his ministry, set forth the doctrine of his mediation and expiatory death? Is there any thing more lucidly stated, or more carefully insisted on in the Bible, than tne gracious work and offices of the Holy Spirit? The foundation will be of no use to us, if we build nothing upon it; and our building is a cloud or a fable—a mere castle in the air—if it does not rest on Christ the Rock of ages.

Persons may entertain very different, and sometimes even opposite views on some other doctrines of religion; which are by no means destitute of importance; and they may be very far from agreeing one with another, either in opinion or practice, in relation to church government and modes of worship; and yet if they thoroughly embrace the sacred truths now adverted to, and hold them in even balances, tracing both these lines of mercy to the fathomless depth of the love of God the Father, they are severally in the way of experiencing the blessed effects of Christianity, so far as relates to its main purpose —the salvation of the soul. Being baptized by the one Spirit into the one needful faith, and being followers of one and the same Lord, they are fellow-members of the one church of Christ upon earth, and may look forward to the perfection of their union in the world to come.

The points on which they differ are unquestionably not to be disregarded. It is greatly to be desired that on these points also, light and truth should spread, and that the simple, broad, spiritual views held out to us in the Holy Scriptures, should be accepted in their native fulness, and primitive strength. Nevertheless, it is an excellent habit of mind—one which we cannot too carefully cherish in ourselves and others—to view the various parts of the fabric of truth *in their right proportions ;* not allowing secondary points, however interesting they may be to ourselves, to occupy a larger portion of our field of vision, than properly belongs to them in the order of the gospel. Such a habit of mind will never discourage us in the faithful support and diligent pursuit of truth; at the same time, it will greatly aid us in the maintenance of that Christian love which is the badge of discipleship. The good old motto was never more important than in the present day of polemical strife and sectarian prejudice, " In essentials, UNITY ; in non-essentials, LIBERTY ; in all things, CHARITY."

It is abundantly evident that we shall never comply with these principles, or form the habit now recommended, while we lean to our own understandings and follow the counsels of our own hearts. Man is by nature prone to dark and distorted views, and there is nothing more common even among persons who make a high profession of religion, than a zeal which is " not according to knowledge." It is only as we are favoured with the help and guidance of the Holy Spirit, and submit to his influence, that we can correctly perceive, and rightly appreciate the various parts of divine truth. There can be no saving knowledge of the gospel of Christ without this influence. "For what man knoweth the things of a man, save the spirit of man which is in him? even so the things of God knoweth no man, but the Spirit of God. Now we have received, not the spirit of the world, but the Spirit which is of God; that we might know the things that are freely given to us of God....... The natural man receiveth not the things of the Spirit of God; ..... neither can he know them, because they are spiritually discerned. But he that is spiritual judgeth (or discerneth, ἀνακρίνει) all things, yet he himself is judged (or discerned, ἀνακρίνεται) of no man. For who hath known the mind of the Lord, that he may instruct him? But we have the mind of Christ."*

"Yes, my brother," said the same pious individual to me in the course of an instructive conversation, "the spiritual man has a sense of his own; or rather, his natural vision is corrected and is rendered applicable to divine things by an influence from above. I am told to look at the planets—I can see Jupiter and Venus; but there is the Georgium Sidus—I look again; I strain my eyes exceedingly, but it is all in vain. 'Here, take the telescope.' 'O yes, now I see it, how

---

* 1 Cor. ii. 11—16.

beautiful the star! how perspicuous the vision!' You tell me to read that almanac. I am young and short-sighted; the ball of my eye is too convex; the rays meet before they arrive at the *retina.* My brother, it is all confusion. I am old—my lens is flattened; the rays meet even behind my head; the retina is left untouched by them. Give the young man those spectacles with a concave glass—now he sees! now he can read the book! now the rays meet precisely on his retina! Here my old friend, take these convex glasses, they will rectify your fading vision. He sees; he reads; again the retina is touched, and pencilled with a nice precision. So it is with the Spirit. In whatsoever manner or degree the soul, or understanding of man, is darkened or diseased, the Spirit is always applicable to our need—always a rectifier."

It is indeed our duty to avail ourselves of every means within our reach, for ascertaining the meaning of Scripture, and for developing its almost endless riches. History, geography, the records of ancient customs, and the testimony of modern travellers—not to mention the critical study of the original languages, and philology in all its legitimate applications—have a very important place as means of an accurate acquaintance with the volume which contains the ever blessed charter of the liberty of souls. Yet that charter may be effectually read and understood by those who have little or no access to these various sources of information: and whether we be numbered among the learned or ignorant of mankind, it is only as we are *habituated*, in the reading of Scripture, to a watchful dependence on the influences of the Spirit—correcting our dispositions and enlightening our vision—that we shall obtain that true and experimental knowledge of religion, on which the value of the book for our substantial improvement and eternal welfare entirely depends.

In order to do justice to the subject now under consideration, we must not attempt to close this essay without some mention of habits more hidden from the observation of men, than the generality of those which we have hitherto noticed, and yet observable enough in their effects—I mean good religious habits of thought, of feeling, of disposition—habits of the rational, responsible soul within us. These, under grace, may be cherished and matured, by education; yet not so much by the care of others, as by that education of ourselves for which we are all responsible in the sight of a just and holy God.

Such habits may be regarded as constituting *frames* of mind—all existing at the same time—co-operating and blending without any interruption of their respective influences—all tending together to the same great end of the happiness of man and the glory of God, while every one manifests itself by its own distinct and peculiar fruits.

1. The first of these habits, or frames of mind, in point of order as well as necessity, is that of the *filial fear of God.*

I am satisfied that even serious Christians are not enough in the practice of impressing this fear on the minds of their children. There is too great a proneness in many parents who know and love the Lord Jesus, and delight themselves in the abundance of the riches which are in Christ, to give to those under their care, a view of all that is joyous and comforting in the Christian system, without communicating to them a full sense of the weight of our responsibilities, the absolute holiness of God, the terribleness of his wrath against every species of iniquity, the certainty of his judgments, the awfulness of his omnipresence, the ever-penetrating eye of his omniscience. But these are parts of the great system of truth, which, beyond all others, perhaps, are of primary importance to the young mind. Youth is too buoyant to be overpowered even by the strongest presentation of these solemn views; yet they are admirably calculated to check its volatility, curb its passions, and restrain its deviations from the paths of virtue; so far as they take possession of the mind, they are ever found, in connexion with conviction for sin, to be the best preparation for a hearty reception of the consolations of the gospel —of the pardoning mercies of God, through Jesus our Lord.

Yet it is truly a filial fear—the fear of the child and not of the slave—which we ought to feel ourselves, and to impress on those whom we educate. The child of God is accustomed to a just view of the moral attributes of the Deity; he loves and reverences that holy law, which is at once the result and expression of those attributes; he trembles at the very notion of sin, which is the transgression of the law—not only because of its penal consequences, but, because he cannot bear to offend that holy and glorious Being, so lovely in his perfections — so adorable in the evidences of his love—whom he has been taught to regard as his Father. Such an one, impressed with reverential fear, can comprehend the full force of those words of prayer, "Our Father which art in heaven—hallowed be thy name— thy kingdom come—thy will be done on earth, as it is in heaven—lead us not into temptation— deliver us from evil!"

2. With this habit of the filial fear of God, is inseparably connected that of *watchfulness.* "Watch and pray, lest ye enter into temptation"— "What I say unto you, I say unto all, Watch." "See that ye walk *circumspectly,* not as fools, but as wise—redeeming the time, because the days are evil."* The word "circumspectly" does not exactly represent the Greek ἀκριβῶς, which rather means *accurately;* yet, in order to walk accurately—that is, in exact accordance with the rule of right—nothing can be more important than the habit of circumspection, or, in other words, the habit of looking *all round* before we take the next step in our walk in life. The mind's eye may easily become accustomed to run this circuit, on every successive occasion, without involving the consequence of a slower pace than would suit the calls either of convenience or duty. The thing required, is, habitual watch-

---

* Matt. xxvi. 41.

fulness of soul before the Lord, by which the Christian traveller may avoid the many snares of the tempter and deceiver of men — " In vain the net is spread in the sight of any bird."* There is such a thing as spiritual *prudence;* there is, also, the restraint or denial of self. These virtues are the sisters of watchfulness, and the parent of them all is the true fear of an Omnipresent, all-wise, and Omnipotent God.

Yet we are not always to expect a clear view of the reasons why one step in the walk of life is preferable to another—why the one is to be taken and the other eschewed—for we walk by faith and not by sight. Happy are those who know how to discern the pointing of the divine finger, and in whom has been formed, through grace, the *Christian habit* of obeying it, even under circumstances of difficulty and darkness. These will walk in their way safely, and if they "follow on," in patience, to know and serve the Lord, they will be sure to verify, in their own experience, the blessed promise of ancient days—
" I will bring the blind by a way that they know not; I will lead them in paths that they have not known: I will make darkness light before them,

---

* Mark xiii. 37.

and crooked things straight. These things will
I do unto them, and not forsake them."* The
eye of faith is opened to behold the directing
hand of the Lord, and subsequent experience will
seldom fail to bring to light those paternal reasons
for such direction, which, for a time, are hidden
under a veil of obscurity. "What I do thou
knowest not now, but thou shalt know hereafter."†

I wish to make myself clear on this interesting
topic. I am not here speaking of what is often
called providential direction—instruction as to the
course which we are to pursue, arising out of the
development of events. I am speaking of the
immediate and perceptible guidance of the Spirit,
which, as I believe, will never be wanting to the
humble, watchful, *waiting* Christian, on all
occasions which involve a moral question, or
which, being temporal and secular in their own
nature, nevertheless affect our spiritual welfare.
I am far from excluding a right use of the
natural faculty of judgment, under that divine
influence by which it is illuminated and rectified.
Yet, beyond the boundaries of this faculty there
is, at times, a walk of *faith* marked out for us,
for which we cannot at present discern the

---

* Isaiah xlii. 16.   † John xiii. 7.

reasons; nevertheless our true safety will be found in implicit and childlike obedience to the dictates of the Spirit. The illustration which the friend, already mentioned, once gave me of this branch of our present subject, is remarkably happy. "The worldling," said he, "is like the mariner of ancient times, who had nothing to guide him through the trackless deep, but the sun, the moon, and the stars: when these were veiled, all was obscurity, guess-work, and peril. But, the true Christian, however simple, is like the modern mariner, who has a compass on board, which will always guide him aright, however cloudy the atmosphere, however dark the night. The Christian has a compass *within him*—a faithful monitor, a clear director. If he consult his compass diligently, he will be sure to form a right decision on every moral question, while the proud philosopher who knows no such teacher, is tossed on the waves of doubt and confusion. And how is this? Why, my dear brother, he is renewed in the *spirit* of his mind. It is because his dispositions are rectified, that his vision is restored."

Of one philosopher, indeed, I have already made mention, who might perhaps be classed among the humble rather than the proud, and who, though a stranger to outwardly revealed truth, was accustomed to consult this modern mariner's compass. I allude to Socrates, that truly great and wise man, who, amidst all the superstition with which he was surrounded, and by which he was himself in some degree infected, gave proofs in his conversation, that he was by no means destitute of a certain measure of divine illumination. But the Christian enjoys far juster views, and far larger experience of the same divine guidance. He sees the pointing of the finger of God; he feels the power which restrains him from all things injurious to his highest welfare; he hears "the still small voice" of the Shepherd of Israel, saying, 'This shalt thou do —and that thou shalt leave UNDONE.' Certain it is that we cannot imbue our children—that we cannot seek to be imbued ourselves—with more important habits, than those of close attention, in the first place, and of implicit obedience in the second, to this guiding, restraining, warning voice of the Spirit of God. It is distinguished from the impulses of human imagination, by the quietness, sobriety, and charity, with which a submission to its dictates never fails to be accompanied. It is the voice of Him who condescends to dwell in his people—of Him, who is infinitely wise, perfectly just and holy, and abounding in mercy and goodness; it commands stillness to the turbulent waves of passion; it leads far away from all that defiles the moral nature of man; it whispers of holy and heavenly things; and after conducting us through paths of deep humiliation, it leaves us to expatiate in the broad fields of piety, truth, and peace. It is that which we see, hear, feel, with the eye, the ear, the nerve of the inmost soul. We know that it comes from our Father, and leads to his eternal abode.

The apostle John, in unison with his Lord and Master, insists on this inward guidance and direction. He ascribes it to the "anointing" which "teacheth" us of "all things, and is truth and no lie."[*] Now the Holy Scriptures themselves, which were given forth under an extraordinary measure of the same divine influence, contain, as we well know, the most explicit and comprehensive statements of the law of the Lord in its various branches. If any man therefore under the pretence or notion of divine guidance, breaks the law of God as it is declared in the Sacred Volume, or contradicts the spirit of that law, such a circumstance affords a

---

[*] 1 John ii. 27.

clear evidence that he is either an impostor or enthusiast. Yet the Scriptures deal in *general* principles—the precepts which they contain apply, with equal force, to all the cases of a class. In the application of any given precept to any particular exigency, we need the immediate teaching of the Holy Spirit, who not only writes the law on the heart, but instructs us, as by a " word behind" us—by a testimony as swift as lightning—how, and when, and where we are to carry it into effect. Happy indeed are they who are *habituated* to a reverent regard for the precepts as well as the doctrines of Holy Writ, and who are equally *accustomed* to hear and obey the " still small voice" of the Spirit of Christ within them! These are truly " the children of the day," who walk not in darkness, but have the "*light* of *life.*"

3. " Put off thy ornaments from thee, that I may know what to do unto thee," was the command given to rebellious Israel in days of old; and the same command, in a spiritual sense, has its vivid application to mankind, under the New Covenant. Putting off our self-righteousness and pride, and all the pomps and vanities of this wicked world, we must resign ourselves to the mighty operation of the hand of God; we must lie passive

under that hand, like the clay under the hand of the potter, that He " may know what to do" with us—that he may form and fashion us as vessels in his house (be our appointed shape what it may) according to his own will and purpose, and for his own use and glory.

There is, perhaps, no habit of mind more wanted among professing Christians, or more desirable in every stage of our religious experience, than that of *passiveness* under the discipline of the cross. This discipline is applied partly through the medium of outward afflictions, and partly by the immediate, sanctifying operations of the Holy Spirit; and without an experience of the latter, the former will be wholly unavailing. "I was dumb with silence, I opened not my mouth, because thou didst it," is an expression of passive submission; and we must endeavour after the state of mind which is thus expressed, not only when the chastening hand of the Lord is laid upon us, in sickness, or other outward affliction, but when he is pleased to baptize us inwardly with the Holy Ghost and with fire—when he burns up the chaff which abounds in the whole internal framework of the natural man, by the heart-searching and heart-cleansing operation of his own Spirit.

Did we know more of this necessary work—did we more patiently abide the furnace of the Lord, during the often prolonged day of humiliation and conflict—were we thus more truly conformed to the sufferings and death of our holy Redeemer—our religion would be of a deeper character, and we should be better prepared to arise out of our low and dark condition, into the true light and liberty of the gospel of Christ.

It would be an unspeakable advantage to the cause of Christianity, were even its serious professors more thoroughly aware, than many of them seem to be at present, that God is not glorified, or his kingdom truly promoted, by performances which do not spring out of the right source, being the offspring of the merely natural working of the mind of man. The grace of God, by which the motives and affections are purified and exalted, and the renovated creature prepared for the uses of the Creator—is the spring of all that is really beneficial for the conversion of sinners, and for the moral and spiritual improvement of mankind. It is a blessed *habit* to wait, and watch, and seek for this grace, and in all our endeavours to promote the welfare of others, as well as our own salvation, to move under its quieting influence, its safe guidance, its dignifying authority. Such a habit would by no means betray us into indolence; but it would often lead us into that wholesome stillness, out of which would arise words fitly spoken in season, and works truly conformed to the will and wisdom of the Lord.

4. Were there less of self—less of the working of man's wild nature—and more of the influence of the Holy Spirit, in our conduct and conversation, there would be a larger, clearer *scope,* for the exercise of another most important mental habit, that of *trusting in God.* Blessed are they who, amidst the ever-varying pleasures, pains, and duties of this shifting scene, can draw near to their invisible yet ever present Protector, with filial confidence—who *habitually* lean on his arm of power, repose on his love and mercy, and steadfastly rely on the stability of his promises. Serving the Lord, walking in the light of his countenance, and depending upon Him under every circumstance, with implicit affiance, such persons possess the secret of true happiness; there is a holy calm over their spirits; they are assured that all things work together for good to them that love God, and that *their* Father doeth all things well; thus they can patiently bear the pains of life, for their darkest hours are gilded

with hope; and they can also taste its innocent pleasures—especially its intimate social joys—with a delightful relish, as those who know that they have no continuing city here, but are seeking one to come.

This mental habit of confidence in God, can never be fully formed in us, unless we believe in the truth as it is in Jesus, and cordially embrace the Saviour, who, being in the form and nature of God, made himself of no reputation, became incarnate in the nature of man, lived as our pattern, died as the propitiation for our sins, rose from the dead, ascended into heaven, sat down at the right hand of the Father, and ever lives to make intercession for us—our holy High Priest —our merciful, sympathizing Head—our glorious Ruler, King, and Judge. It is impossible for us too strongly to impress upon the minds of young people, the value and excellence of that mighty plan of redemption, which is unfolded to us in Holy Writ, or too carefully to cherish in them the blessed *habit* of seeking access to the Father THROUGH THE SON. A just view of the mediatorial offices of Christ—a heartfelt faith in Jesus as the Saviour of the world—will render their *trust in God* intelligent and stable; they will comprehend the reason why, notwithstanding their great weakness and unworthiness, and their many past transgressions, they may *nevertheless* approach God with confidence, and rely on his matchless love and goodness. Broken and humbled though they be—and broken and humbled they *must* be, if they would approach him *availingly*—they discover that there is no ground for discouragement or despair; and thus are they prepared to run their appointed race with a holy alacrity. Nor will this alacrity be weakened as they gain experience, and grow old in the knowledge and service of Christ. Though their sensations may then be less vivid than in the days of their youth, their principles will become more deeply rooted, more strongly confirmed; their trust in God through Jesus Christ will be more settled; and when, at last, they shall find themselves passing through the valley of the shadow of death, they will fear no evil, because God is with them; and peaceful will be their strong though humble hope—their quiet, unwavering assurance—that they shall dwell in the house of the Lord FOR EVER.

> "What though, as years roll on and shift the scene,
> A calmer, cooler mood may supervene,
> Yet spreads the root in the deep soil below,
> And riper fruits on firmer branches grow;
> Well tempered charity, substantial peace,
> Wisdom and fortitude with years increase;

> Patience to suffer, meekness to forbear,
> With nice discernment of each hidden snare;
> The watchful eye, the ever deepening sense
> Of man's defect, and God's omnipotence;
> The chastened heart oft prostrate in the dust,
> The stedfast walking, the UNBENDING TRUST,
> And hope well settled on the joys above,
> The calm reflection of a Saviour's love;
> To perfect day, the just man's path shall shine,
> Thou Holy Comforter, its light is THINE."

5. When the spies who were sent to examine the land of Canaan, brought back to the camp of Israel their vast bunches of grapes, with a terrible report of the Anakim who dwelt in that country, they were justly liable to rebuke and punishment. The hopes excited by the luscious fruit were overturned by the terrors of their gloomy tale, and the people of God were discouraged from pursuing their arduous pilgrimage. It is worthy of consideration whether those Christians are not liable to similar blame, who, while they sometimes insist on the delights of that spiritual kingdom which "is not meat nor drink, but righteousness, and peace, and joy in the Holy Ghost," are for the most part, so clad in sackcloth, and so obviously appalled by the conflicts which attend their course, that they give a bad report of heavenly things to all around

them, and minister discouragement to many a weary pilgrim—to many a seeking soul.

Reconciled to God, through faith in Jesus Christ, and united by the same faith to Him who is exalted far above all principality and power, at the right hand of the Father, the Christian is bound to obey the apostolic precept, "Rejoice evermore; in every thing give thanks." He ought surely, to show to his fellow-men, not only that the virtues which are the fruit of true religion, are pleasant and wholesome, but also that the giants who "dwell in the land," are often nothing better than shadows, and when giants indeed, are under the absolute control of that Saviour, whose covenant of light and life ensures both the present safety, and the ultimate victory of his followers. The result of an habitual attention to this bright but just view of the subject, will be a serenity of soul equally habitual; and this serenity will manifest itself in a cheerful demeanour and happy countenance. These will speak a language of their own, which may be interpreted by the words, Come and " have fellowship with us; for truly our fellowship is with the Father and with his Son Jesus Christ."* Undoubtedly there will occur to

---
* 1 John i. 3.

the Christian, times of spiritual fasting, as well as feasting. At such times, let us *accustom ourselves* to act on the spirit of our Saviour's injunction: "But thou, when thou fastest, anoint thy head, and wash thy face, that thou appear not unto men to fast, but unto thy Father which seeth in secret, and thy Father which seeth in secret, shall reward thee openly."*

It was said by a prophet, in days of old, that "they who feared the Lord spake often one to another; and the Lord hearkened, and heard it, and a book of remembrance was written before him for them that feared the Lord, and that thought upon his name."† A painful reserve on the most interesting and important of all subjects is sometimes to be remarked, even in persons who are by no means destitute of pious feelings. Such a reserve spreads an icy influence, which is little calculated to promote a generous ardour for truth and righteousness in the minds of the young and inexperienced. Others, on the contrary, are too frequent and familiar in their *talk* on serious subjects; and that which is in itself unspeakably precious and cheering becomes, through their untutored zeal, both dry and unpalatable. There

---

* Matt. vi. 17. † Malachi iii. 16.

is in this matter a "golden mean," which parents, tutors, and religious friends cannot too carefully observe. "Out of the abundance of the heart the mouth speaketh;" and the subject of religion ought never to be handled, even in social conversation, except under a lively feeling of its supreme importance, and in such a manner as to promote the same feeling in those with whom we are conversing. "Let your speech be always with grace, *seasoned with salt.*"*

6. Of all the characteristics of the "old man, which is corrupt according to the deceitful lusts," none are more prominent, or more universal, than the inordinate love of self—a love manifested in a thousand different forms, and always accompanied by a corresponding absence of love to God. Nor is there any part of the experience of the new creature in Christ, so essential to his character and his hopes, as "the *expulsive* power of a new affection,"—even of that love for our Creator and Redeemer, which drives out the love of self, and of the world, from our bosoms.

When we contemplate the perfections of God, as they are displayed in the works of nature, in

---

* Col. iv. 6.

the order of Providence, and especially in the Holy Scriptures, we cannot fail to learn, that he is supremely worthy, not only of our filial fear and reverence, but of our fervent, constant love; nor can we avoid acknowledging the justness of the first and great commandment, " Thou shalt love the Lord thy God with all thy heart, and with all thy mind, and with all thy strength." More especially when our Christianity becomes vital and truly intelligent—when " God, who commanded the light to shine out of darkness, hath shined in our hearts, to give us the light of the knowledge of the glory of God, in the face of Jesus Christ"—we cannot do otherwise, than love Him who " FIRST LOVED US." The gift of his only begotten Son to be the Propitiation for our sins, and the Saviour of the world, is the highest evidence of our Heavenly Father's love. The Son himself, also, in his own boundless benevolence and charity, herein co-operates with the Father, to whose will he is subject. " He hath loved" us, and " given HIMSELF" for us. Nor are we to forget the love of the Holy Ghost, the Comforter, who visits the degraded and benighted children of men, and richly dwells, as the very source of purity and peace, in the hearts of the Lord's children. Penetrated with a view of the height, and depth, and length, and breadth of this divine love, the heart of the believer will be for ever fixed, in reverent gratitude and fervent affection, on the Father, Son, and Spirit—ONE GOD BLESSED FOR EVERMORE.

When this love to God becomes an habitual principle of action, it imparts a holy decision of character; it gently constrains to an unreserved surrender of the soul; our faith works by it, and by every act of obedience which that faith produces, it is more and more enlarged and strengthened. So comprehensive is its character, that springing up to God, in the first place, it again descends as a mighty stream from his heavenly throne, and encircles the earth below; so that a genuine love to the Supreme Being, never fails to bring along with it, a fervent love for our brethren also, and that blessed charity which embraces the whole family of man. Those who are animated by this divine affection, will be ever bearing the pleasant fruits of integrity, justice, purity, and universal kindness; they will follow the example of a perfect Saviour; and they will be qualified, far above the wise of this world, to be good citizens of the city which continueth not—good members of that vast community of rational beings who are placed on the earth, under the natural and moral government of the Creator of the universe.

This, certainly, is one great point to be always considered in the formation of good *religious* habits, which are of primary importance, as a qualification for the claims and purposes of the present life. They are associated in friendly union, with good habits of body, of art, and of intellect, pervading and elevating them all. With good moral habits they are connected in the peculiar relation which the root bears to the fruit; they are, in fact, the development of that work of grace, which can alone enable corrupt and degraded man truly to fulfil the varied obligations which attach to his mortal existence.

Nevertheless, we must always remember that "our conversation (i. e., our citizenship — πολιτευμα) is in heaven, from whence also we look for the Saviour, the Lord Jesus Christ."* Never must we forget that it is the gracious purpose of our Creator, during the whole course of this present life, to educate us for ETERNITY. All the pleasures which we enjoy, all the pains which we suffer, all the temptations to which we are exposed all our calls of duty and business, all the

---

* Phil. iii. 20, 21.

claims on our benevolence and good-doing, all our social affections and relations, all the interlaced machinery of circumstances and events, with which we come in contact—even the very evils which surround us—constitute a *school of discipline*, in which the Holy Spirit of our God (if we do but believe and obey) will lead, teach, and train us, that so we may be prepared for an infinitely higher and happier world—a world of endless bliss, and perfect purity.

The scenes of sorrow and joy, of duty, business, and pleasure, which here occupy so much of our attention, will soon pass away. The shadows of life flit before us for a moment, and then vanish for ever. The anxious and often turbulent dream, in which we are now involved, will presently be dispelled by the wakening ray of the morning. "The night is far spent"—"the day"—the eternal day—"is at hand." Let us then, in reverent dependence on divine grace, yet with holy resolution and diligence, cultivate the habit of *heavenly mindedness*. Let us "seek those things which are above, where Christ sitteth at the right hand of God." Let us fight "the good fight of faith," and "lay hold of eternal life." Let us press onward through every difficulty, humiliation, temptation, and sorrow, until we shall finally exchange the CROSS which we bear after Jesus, for a CROWN immortal, incorruptible, and full of glory.

THE END.

www.ingramcontent.com/pod-product-compliance
Lightning Source LLC
Chambersburg PA
CBHW022055230426
43672CB00008B/1183